Editor-in-Chief and Founder:
Lyndon H. LaRouche, Jr.
Editorial Board: *Lyndon H. LaRouche, Jr. , Helga
Zepp-LaRouche, Robert Ingraham, Tony
Papert, Gerald Rose, Dennis Small, Jeffrey
Steinberg, William Wertz*
Co-Editors: *Robert Ingraham, Tony Papert*
Managing Editor: *Nancy Spannaus*
Technology: *Marsha Freeman*
Books: *Katherine Notley*
Ebooks: *Richard Burden*
Graphics: *Alan Yue*
Photos: *Stuart Lewis*
Circulation Manager: *Stanley Ezrol*

INTELLIGENCE DIRECTORS
Counterintelligence: *Jeffrey Steinberg, Michele
Steinberg*
Economics: *John Hoefle, Marcia Merry Baker,
Paul Gallagher*
History: *Anton Chaitkin*
Ibero-America: *Dennis Small*
Russia and Eastern Europe: *Rachel Douglas*
United States: *Debra Freeman*

INTERNATIONAL BUREAUS
Bogotá: *Miriam Redondo*
Berlin: *Rainer Apel*
Copenhagen: *Tom Gillesberg*
Houston: *Harley Schlanger*
Lima: *Sara Madueño*
Melbourne: *Robert Barwick*
Mexico City: *Gerardo Castilleja Chávez*
New Delhi: *Ramtanu Maitra*
Paris: *Christine Bierre*
Stockholm: *Ulf Sandmark*
United Nations, N.Y.C.: *Leni Rubinstein*
Washington, D.C.: *William Jones*
Wiesbaden: *Göran Haglund*

ON THE WEB
e-mail: eirns@larouchepub.com
www.larouchepub.com
www.executiveintelligencereview.com
www.larouchepub.com/eiw
Webmaster: *John Sigerson*
Assistant Webmaster: *George Hollis*
Editor, Arabic-language edition: *Hussein Askary*

EIR (ISSN 0273-6314) *is published weekly
(50 issues), by EIR News Service, Inc.,
P.O. Box 17390, Washington, D.C. 20041-0390.
(703) 297-8434*

European Headquarters: E.I.R. GmbH, Postfach
Bahnstrasse 9a, D-65205, Wiesbaden, Germany
Tel: 49-611-73650
Homepage: http://www.eir.de
e-mail: info@eir.de
Director: Georg Neudecker

Montreal, Canada: 514-461-1557
eir@eircanada.ca

Denmark: EIR - Danmark, Sankt Knuds Vej 11,
basement left, DK-1903 Frederiksberg, Denmark.
Tel.: +45 35 43 60 40, Fax: +45 35 43 87 57. e-mail:
eirdk@hotmail.com.

Mexico City: EIR, Sor Juana Inés de la Cruz 242-2
Col. Agricultura C.P. 11360
Delegación M. Hidalgo, México D.F.
Tel. (5525) 5318-2301
eirmexico@gmail.com

Canada Post Publication Sales Agreement
#40683579

Postmaster: Send all address changes to *EIR*, P.O.
Box 17390, Washington, D.C. 20041-0390.

Signed articles in *EIR* represent the views of the authors,
and not necessarily those of the Editorial Board.

The Presidency and the Future of Mankind

EIR Contents

www.larouchepub.com Volume 44, Number 51, December 22, 2017

Cover This Week

Apollo 15 astronaut Jim Irwin salutes the American flag while standing beside the Lunar Module and rover, July 31, 1971.

THE PRESIDENCY AND THE FUTURE OF MANKIND

To Crush the Assault On the Presidency

by Barbara Boyd

Dec. 16—The past week saw the first widespread exposure of the corrupt use of federal agencies, particularly the FBI, in the "palace coup" aspects of the ongoing attempt to topple President Trump. As sordid as the actions of a James Comey-led cabal of FBI agents have been revealed to be, if those involved in insurrection are to be fully exposed and prosecuted, Congress must dig deeper.

If the American people are to rally to the President's side, they need a better understanding of the motives for the attempted coup against Trump. They also must see fundamental economic progress, which, if it happens, will finally deal the ongoing coup attempt a fatal blow.

That is why LaRouche PAC has set a deadline of the President's State of the Union address on Jan. 30, 2018, to end this coup attempt, to secure U.S. participation in China's great One Belt One Road project, and to see Lyndon LaRouche's Four Laws for the economic recovery of the United States introduced as a national legislative program.

In this article, we expand and update materials first set out in the *EIR* Special Report, "Robert Mueller is an Amoral Legal Assassin: He Will Do His Job If You Let Him." Here we provide further evidence of the British origins of the coup, by highlighting the central role in

the coup against Trump being played by the Anglo-American intelligence network. The same network also saw prominent "action" in the British-led, Obama-implemented, 2013-2014 *coup d'état* in Ukraine. This is not an accident. We also detail the desperate and crazed intervention of former President Barack Obama's intelligence chiefs in a bogus lawsuit presently pending in U.S. District Court in Washington, D.C., against the

FBI

U.S. Army/Sgt. Amanda Moncada

Some of the cabal of officials and former officials Special Counsel Robert Mueller (above) is using in his campaign to topple President Trump: (left to right) Andrew McCabe, Deputy Director of the FBI, Nellie Ohr, formerly of the CIA, and Bruce Ohr, Deputy Associate Attorney General at the Department of Justice.

Trump Campaign and Roger Stone. This intervention, aimed at intimidating a sitting U.S. District Court Judge, was and is designed to resurrect the Russiagate narrative which has been uniformly rejected by the American public. Keeping this insane narrative going is central to continuing Robert Mueller's Special Counsel investigation, which rests on highly dubious legal foundations.

The Immediate Big News

By any account, the revelations which came out this week concerning FBI Agent Peter Strzok, his mistress FBI Attorney Lisa Page, and the Ohr family—he high up in the U.S. Department of Justice, she a former CIA agent working for Fusion GPS—would be big news. On Dec. 2, the day after former National Security Advisor Michael Flynn pled guilty to lying to the FBI, both the *Washington Post* and the *New York Times* received leaks to the effect that Peter Strzok, the FBI case agent for the Russia investigation of the Trump Campaign and the Trump transition, had been removed from Robert Mueller's investigative team in July 2017, due to obvious political bias. According to the leaks, evidence of Strzok's anti-Trump bias was found by the Justice Department Inspector General in text messages exchanged between Strzok and Lisa Page, both members of Robert Mueller's prosecutorial team.

The text messages between Strzok and Page had been divulged to Robert Mueller and Deputy Attorney General Rod Rosenstein in July. On the evening of Dec. 12, a small sampling of the texts was released to the news media by the Department of Justice. And boy, these texts are something else! On Aug. 6, 2016, Page informs Strzok that it is his duty to protect the country from that "menace," meaning Donald Trump. She links her message to a David Brooks article in the *New York Times,* which counsels, "if you're not in revolt you're in cahoots. When this period and your name are mentioned, decades hence, your grandkids will look away in shame." On Aug. 26, 2016, Strzok tells Page he has visited a Walmart in southern Virginia and, "I could *smell* the Trump support ... it's scary down there." The most significant text released concerns an apparent meeting among Strzok, Page, and other senior FBI of-

Peter Strzok

ficials. Page writes: "I want to believe the path you threw out for consideration in Andy's office—that there's no way he gets elected *but I'm afraid we can't take that risk.*" Strzok writes back, *"It's like an insurance policy in the unlikely event you die before you're 40."*

At the time of these text messages, Strzok was Comey's lead case agent on both the Clinton email case and the unprecedented Trump/Russia investigation. The latter counterintelligence investigation was opened in July 2016, based on a dirty dossier written by British MI6 agent Christopher Steele and circulated in the United States by his business partner, Fusion GPS. Both Strzok and Page worked under "Andy" or Andrew McCabe, the Deputy Director of the FBI.

McCabe had his own Clinton-bias problem: His wife Jill ran for the Virginia State Senate, and her major donors were top Hillary Clinton presidential campaign bundlers who joined the Clinton family's former chief fundraiser, Virginia Governor Terry McAuliffe, to support her campaign. McCabe participated in both the money meeting and his wife's campaign, in probable violation of the Hatch Act. It is probable that the investigation and leaking of Christopher Steele's dirty dossier against Donald Trump is the "insurance policy" being discussed in these texts.

It was Strzok who interviewed Michael Flynn at the White House in January 2017 after Andrew McCabe set Flynn up, by only telling him that the FBI needed to talk to him about some intelligence matter, and never warning him that it was a full-scale criminal interview in which Flynn was the target. Ambushed, Flynn sat down with Strzok without a lawyer. Strzok had the full National Security Agency (NSA) transcripts of Flynn's conversations with Russian Ambassador Sergey Kislyak to guide his questions. Flynn struggled to remember the details of telephone conversations which had occurred while he was on a family vacation. Flynn apparently flunked the memory test. Even James Comey did not think, however, that Flynn *intentionally* lied. He told the House Intelligence Committee on March 4, 2017, that Flynn had simply forgotten things. It is in the nature of our Torquemada, Robert Mueller, that the exculpatory

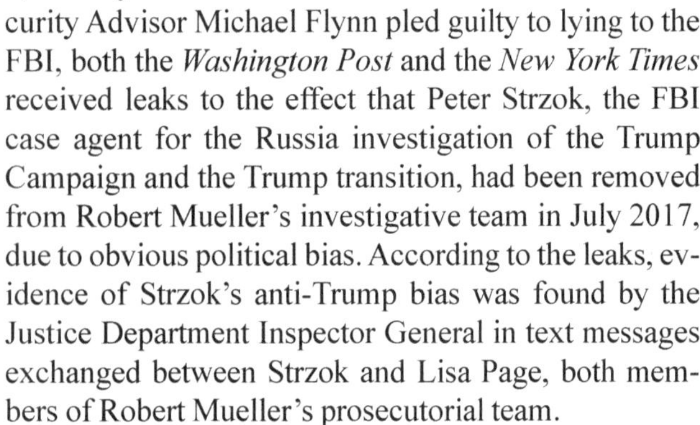

information about the bias of the FBI agent who interviewed Flynn, and the circumstances of that interview, were kept from public view until after Mueller secured Michael Flynn's scalp and ruined his life.

Strzok most certainly met Christopher Steele, and, in all probability, played a major role in writing the dubious and fact-free January U.S. intelligence community "assessment" that the Russians hacked the DNC and John Podesta, and otherwise meddled in the U.S. election to the benefit of Donald Trump. Strzok was considered to be the FBI's leading expert on Russia.

As this was unfolding, the Department of Justice confirmed that Deputy Associate Attorney General Bruce Ohr had been demoted because of unauthorized contacts with Christopher Steele and Glenn Simpson of Fusion GPS. Ohr's wife, Nellie Ohr, it turns out, was hired by Fusion GPS to gather dirt on Donald Trump. Nellie Ohr, Bruce Ohr, Lisa Page, Peter Strzok, Christopher Steele, and Glenn Simpson of Fusion GPS have all been closely associated in joint Anglo-American intelligence efforts allegedly directed at investigating organized crime, corruption, and money-laundering in the former East Bloc, an association shared with Andrew McCabe. It is an enterprise wholly penetrated and controlled by British intelligence.

Separate from this drama, Freedom Works, a Washington, D.C.-based advocacy group, announced that it had obtained an email under the Freedom of Information Act, in which Mueller's chief prosecutorial bulldog, Andrew Weissmann, expressed his awe and admiration for Deputy Attorney General Sally Yates for telling the entire Justice Department to "stand down" and not argue for enforcement of the President's travel order, restricting travel to the United States from certain countries. Clearly, the "resistance movement" permeates the present ranks of the Department of Justice.

Xinhua

Xinhua/Michael Teweldi

China's development drive in Africa, which will greatly expand with its Belt and Road Initiative, is creating an unprecedented optimism there. Three of China's projects are shown here. Top left, Chinese-built passenger rail in Addis Ababa, Ethiopia; top right, construction site in Awassa, Ethiopia; below, a hydro-electric power station in Cote d'Ivoire.

Xinhua

The President's supporters now finally smell blood in their efforts to defeat the coup attempt. Actually defeating it, however, requires an appropriate counterintelligence focus.

Lyndon LaRouche uses the principle of the transfinite to define strategic reality. What are the defining principles of the present strategic situation? What are the actual forces which are moving history as new ideas come into physical being? What are the transformative effects of those ideas? LaRouche specifies that China's initiative, in alliance with Russia and 110 other nations, to develop Eurasia and large swaths of the presently underdeveloped world on a completely new physical-economic platform, with focused intentions to explore and develop space, has fundamentally transformed all human relationships, including all strategic relationships.

Africa, for the first time in recent history, is seeing actual physical economic development as a result—a platform of connected transportation, new cities, new manufacturing plants, and new dams and waterways.

Building housing the MI6 headquarters in London.

Aerial view of the GCHQ in Cheltenham, Gloucestershire.

this framework. If you can't understand why the British and their friends in the Obama Administration set out to first defeat and then regime-change Donald Trump, you won't be able to locate and prosecute the actual leaders of the insurrection. You'll get lost in the whirlwind of details and particulars, blinding you to the larger picture. The British intervention into the U.S. election, led by Christopher Steele, MI6, and General Communications Headquarters (GCHQ), and beginning in 2015, was caused by Trump's stubborn and righteous refusal to continue the deluded war-drive launched by the British and Barack Obama in response to China's great One Belt One Road (OBOR) infrastructure development proposals. OBOR was viewed, falsely, as an existential threat to their continued world dominance. That war drive itself began in 2013-2014 with the Obama Administration's *coup d'état* in Ukraine. It is no accident that key actors in the present coup attempt played a significant role in Ukraine, and that key themes employed there, including alleged Russian mastery of mind-bending propaganda, have also played a major role in the ongoing criminal coup attempt against Trump.

Russia! Russia! Russia!

Robert Mueller's investigative mandate, set forth in a May 17, 2017 letter from Acting Attorney General Rod Rosenstein, specifies that Mueller is supposed to be investigating the claim that the Trump campaign "colluded" with Putin, the GRU, and the successors to the KGB to defeat Hillary Clinton. There is absolutely no legal authority, under the Special Counsel regulations, for a Special Counsel to conduct such an ill-defined counterintelligence investigation. Under the regulations, Special Counsels are only supposed to investigate specifically defined federal crimes, in situations where the Department of Justice has a conflict of interest. If the primary predicate for the FBI's Russia investigation, the Steele dossier, is bogus, then Mueller's already shaky legal authority to investigate is bogus. Hence the recent frantic attempt to put lipstick on a pig, resurrect Christopher Steele's credibility, and repackage the "red menace." One big step in this

Similar efforts are underway throughout the formerly colonial world. The elimination of poverty is posed for the first time as a realistic target with a due date. With development comes hope, optimism, and creativity.

Meanwhile, the West continues to wallow in the old decadent post-industrial paradigm where a very small percentage of the population gets rich, science and technology stagnate, and regimes with "no future" are sustained by instant gratifications, whether they be in tribal identity political wars, mind-numbing popular entertainments, pornography, or drugs. The West has absolutely nothing similar to the optimism of China's Initiative, to offer its citizens. It can only maintain power by surveillance, mass-media brainwashing which sets the terms of popular debate, and, if it comes to it, force.

Defeating the coup attempt means situating it within

massively funded PR effort is a new book just out about Christopher Steele. Another is the bizarre intervention by Obama's intelligence chiefs, in the bogus lawsuit (Case No. 1:17-cv-1370-ESH) brought by Obama's lawyers against the Trump Campaign and Roger Stone, now pending in the U.S. District Court for the District of Columbia.

The sensational, trashy allegations of the Steele dossier have been under investigation for months. No one has yet been able to prove them. Even the fake news media found them incredible when they were leaked during the campaign. Even Steele himself does not stand by their veracity, noting that they constitute raw, unverified intelligence from his former MI6 assets, often in third- and fourth-hand reports. Steele's sources are a network of compromised Russians, Ukrainians, and others who are totally dependent for their continued existence on making a good impression on MI6. We now know that Hillary Clinton and the Democratic National Committee paid for Steele's dossier on Trump and systematically leaked it to journalists to defeat then candidate Trump. Some of the journalists appear to have been paid for this service.

It also seems clear that James Comey and senior leadership at the FBI, including Strzok, McCabe, et al., dressed up allegations produced by Steele, paid for by Hillary Clinton, the DNC—and, in all probability, by MI6 and the FBI—into more consequential legalese, and peddled them to the Foreign Intelligence Surveillance Act (FISA) court and other surveillance authorities as part of an unprecedented counterintelligence operation against Donald Trump's presidential campaign. An FBI counterintelligence investigation is always aimed at "neutralization" of a target. It uses classified and otherwise illegal tactics. In this case, the Steele dossier was the pretext to employ these methods against a U.S. presidential candidate, an unprecedented abuse of the FBI's powers.

The public side of the campaign to redeem Steele centers on a book about him by MI6-connected "journalist" Luke Harding. Harding's book, *Collusion: How Russia Helped Trump Win the White House*, has been the subject of documentaries by Rachel Maddow on MSNBC and puff pieces in all the main-stream news media. It presents Steele as a recognized authority on Russia who

is viewed with gravitas by every major intelligence agency in the world, despite the fact that he completely flopped in his initial appearance before a discerning American public. Despite its intention, the book provides major clues about the British coup attempt against Trump, if the reader is operating from the right strategic dimension.

According to Harding, Christopher Steele played an instrumental role in the British/Barack Obama directed 2013-2014 *coup d'état* in Ukraine, drafting over a hundred intelligence memos for Victoria Nuland at the State Department and Secretary of State John Kerry. Nuland was the U.S. case officer for the Ukraine coup. According to Harding, Steele used the same sources for his Ukraine memos as he used for the Trump dirty dossier.

Harding also identifies the longstanding business ties between Christopher Steele and Glenn Simpson's Fusion GPS, the United States Department of Justice, and the FBI. Fusion GPS's lucrative business relationship with Steele consists of developing trash for pay—opposition research for different oligarch clients in Russia and the former East Bloc who perpetually war with one another. It is the perfect cover for British and American intelligence penetration of the entire area. Steele's longstanding FBI contacts, according to Harding, are primarily in the Eurasian Organized Crime Strike Force, an organization long associated with FBI Deputy Director Andrew McCabe and supervised by Bruce Ohr.

The Ukraine Connection

Most of the claptrap sold to the American public about Russian propaganda and hybrid-warfare efforts originated with the coup in Ukraine. According to this fake narrative and the absurd "assessment" of the U.S. intelligence community, the Russians are super-good propagandists, with the mastermind, Vladimir Putin, fine-tuning the details daily. Putin is consistently portrayed as a cartoon-like villain from a James Bond novel in these vignettes—think Bond-supervillain Ernst Stavro Blofeld. Russian-connected television channels and publications with small audiences, such as RT and Sputnik, are claimed to punch orders of magnitude above their weight, according to this British intelligence-originated narrative, exerting a huge and de-

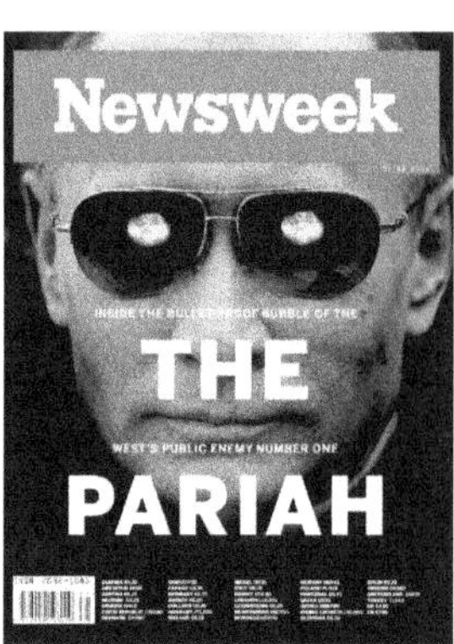

Examples of the media effort to villify Russian President Putin as an evil schemer.

monic influence. Somehow Putin has found a magic formula to infect the American mind and spread the infection. The Russians, it is claimed, were able to use a minuscule social media effort (when compared to the 2016 presidential campaigns and PACs) to somehow make race, police violence, or similar issues, brand-new and hugely divisive concerns in the United States.

Politico Magazine on Nov. 15, 2017, recounted a telephone call between Hillary Clinton and Rick Stengel, who, as head of the State Department's Public Diplomacy desk, was a propaganda chief in U.S. regime-change operations. The call took place on a Saturday morning in 2014, four weeks after Putin "annexed" Crimea and long after Clinton had left office. Clinton heatedly complained that the United States was losing the propaganda war to Russia over Ukraine—that the State Department was "issuing press releases" while Putin was "rewriting history." Sharing Clinton's view, the British and NATO set up huge military and psychological warfare operations to "neutralize" the Russian view and ensure it didn't reach American eyes and ears. A big part of this effort was spreading the Ernst Stavro Blofeld black-hat image of Putin throughout the world. A second feature, to ensure high levels of funding for U.S. propaganda efforts, required portraying Russian news and propaganda efforts as some sort of all-powerful monster apparat. Prominently featured, since 2014, in ensuing British-generated propaganda, is the so-called St. Petersburg Internet Research Agency. If Russian intelligence is so infinitely clever, why would they use the same photographed building for hacking and social-media bot generation over a three-year period after it had been exposed? The answer should be obvious. They didn't.

The Ukrainian-American, Alexandra Chalupa, figures prominently in the fake DNC hacking story and the case of former Trump campaign manager, Paul Manafort. Chalupa worked directly with Ukrainian intelligence to dig up dirt on Manafort, collaborated with journalist Michael Isikoff in that effort, and was paid $412,000 for this and similar "work." Isikoff was also shopped the Steele dossier by his long-time friend Glenn Simpson of Fusion GPS. Mueller indicted Manafort not for his "Russian" collusion but for his earlier activities on behalf of the loser in the U.S.-run Ukrainian coup, Viktor Yanukovych. Lisa Page, Peter Strzok's extra-marital lover, is reported to have played a key role in the FBI investigation of one of Manafort's business partners, Ukrainian oligarch Dmitry Firtash, during the same period.

DNC "opposition researcher" Alexandra Chalupa, it is claimed, discovered the hacking of the DNC by the Russians when she began receiving strange security warnings from Yahoo on her DNC computer while engaged in espionage against Trump and Manafort. The individual called in to diagnose the alleged hack was Dmitri Alperovitch, co-founder and chief technology officers of CrowdStrike, a violently anti-Putin Russian expat otherwise involved in the MI6/CIA end of anti-Russian propaganda operations in Ukraine. As readers of this publication know, the "hacking" of the DNC by the Russians did not occur. This has been proven by the studies of the Veteran Intelligence Professionals for Sanity (VIPS) and articulated by William Binney, a former NSA Technical Director. Alexandra Chalupa, her sister Andrea Chalupa, and her mother Irene Chalupa, a longstanding State Department propagandist, all participated heavily in the Ukraine coup itself, running an operation called "Digital Maidan," which included sloganeering dear to the ears of the Neo-Nazi Alt Right sector which served as the coup's military wing. The Ukrainian neo-Nazis have been British and CIA assets since the end of World War II.

Those Republicans chasing the "Uranium One" phantom would be wise to actually examine the leading contributors to the Clinton Foundation since Hillary left the State Department. They are Ukraine, England, and the Saudis, in that order, with Ukrainian oligarch Victor Pinchuk playing the lead role.

Director of National Intelligence James Clapper (center), FBI Director James Comey (left), and CIA Director John Brennan (right) at the Senate Select Committee on Intelligence, Feb. 9, 2017.

As part of the Obama Administration's hybrid warfare against Russia, the Justice Department's organized and transnational crime units have played a significant role. These units and corresponding units in the FBI, such as the Eurasian Organized Crime Strike Force, are the very units now implicated in the coup operation against Trump. The DOJ's legal-assassins-with-briefcases have been deployed repeatedly, using corruption charges and associated media psywar campaigns, to take out political figures throughout the world who have earned Anglo-American disfavor.

A good start to exposing the deeper foundations of the coup attempt against Trump, then, consists of continuing to "peel the onion" on the Steele dossier and its use by Obama's FBI, Justice Department, and intelligence chiefs. Congress is being stonewalled by Robert Mueller and Deputy Attorney General Rod Rosenstein on its questions concerning the Steele dossier, and this stonewall is presently the subject of a contempt of Congress claim being prepared by the House Intelligence Committee, against Attorney General Sessions and Rod Rosenstein. The President should consider ordering the Justice Department to declassify the materials sought by Congress, explaining to the American people why doing so is a matter of national security. A second investigative track should involve a security review of those occupying the various Eurasian and Russian desks in the State Department, Justice Department, and the rest of the intelligence community—during the Obama years and presently—starting with those actively involved in the Ukraine coup. What has their role been in the illegal leak campaign against Donald Trump?

Reds Under Every Bed

It is a feature of what news aggregator Matt Drudge calls the "Too Much Crazy" which dominates present U.S. life, that what would, in former times, be taken as slapstick comedy, now assumes funereal tones of dead seriousness. Such is the case with the Obama intelligence community's Dec. 8 intervention into the bogus lawsuit filed against the Trump Campaign and Roger Stone. It is a blatant demonstration of the political bias of Obama's intelligence chiefs, and their singular madness about Putin and Russia. Clearly, this was not limited to the FBI. The *Amicus* intervention and accompanying publicity is also another attempt to resurrect the flagging "Russian meddling in the election" narrative central to Robert Mueller's investigative mandate.

The lawsuit (*Cockrum et al. v. Trump for President & Stone*) claims that the Trump Campaign and Stone collaborated with Russians and WikiLeaks to publish (supposedly hacked) emails from the DNC, and that three individuals named in the "hacked" material suffered damage because their personal information and emails were exposed to public view. As an example of the weakness of the case, one of the named plaintiffs, who had openly claimed he was gay to friends and colleagues, claims that the WikiLeaks publication resulted in his grandmother figuring out he was gay. The lawyers bringing the lawsuit are associated with non-profit United to Protect Democracy, composed of former White House and Obama Administration lawyers. The group was formed, according to *Politico*, as a "worst case scenario" group to tackle Trump. It is funded by George Soros-linked groups, and proposes to conduct a civil legal war against the Trump Administration. In their statements about this case, the Obama lawyers have said that they intend to survive a motion to dismiss and gain discovery on their phony claims. Having read the record in this case, it is clear to any legally informed observer that this lawsuit could not survive the present motion to dismiss in any federal court in the United States. Changing that result appears to be the purpose of the intervention by Obama's intelligence chiefs, who are attempting to coerce a U.S. District Court Judge into creating a plausible cause of action where there is none, based on who they are, the threat they represent, and a completely fabricated and paranoid legend concerning the strength of Russian subversion operations.

Claiming not to take a position on behalf of either party, the *Amici* (friends of the court) write that they have intervened in this lawsuit to offer the Court a "broad perspective on a specific question of national security that may bear on the Court's consideration of the case—whether and how Russia uses local actors inside a country to facilitate disinformation campaigns. Active Measures campaigns encompass a range of activities that include written and spoken disinformation, the spreading of conspiracy theories, efforts to control the media, the use of forgeries, political influence campaigns, the funding of extremist and opposition groups, and cyberattacks."

They then go on to detail a variety of claimed Russian active measures operations dating back to the Reagan Administration, while failing to tell the Court that the United States began a far better funded and resourced Active Measures campaign, directed from the White House by the CIA's Walter Raymond Jr., against Russia at that time. Working with Roy Godson, Herbert Romerstein, and other persons associated with the paranoid and mad James Jesus Angleton—whose British-inspired Russian

U.S. State Department

William Burns

U.S. State Department

Michael McFaul

CIA

Michael Morell

wikipedia

Michael V. Hayden

mole hunt devastated U.S. intelligence capabilities for a generation—Raymond's operation aimed to destroy anyone in the way of U.S. geopolitical goals. Lyndon LaRouche was a principal target of this operation.

The *Amici* rant on: "Throughout, a hallmark of Russian active measures has been its reliance on intermediaries or 'cut outs' inside a country to facilitate active measure campaigns. Those actors include political organizers and activists, academics, journalists, web operators, shell companies, nationalists and militant groups, and prominent pro-Russia businessmen. They range from the unwitting accomplice who is manipulated to act in what he believes is his best interest, to the ideological or economic ally who broadly shares Russian interests, to the knowing agent of influence. The use of these intermediaries is designed to amplify the scope and reach of Russian influence while hiding their involvement." So here's the actual message of the Amicus Brief and Obama's mad intelligence chiefs: There are reds under every bed, folks, and you just don't appreciate it, but we do. The evidence, as always, is classified. Even if no one can prove that the Russians intervened in the U.S. election or that Stone and the Trump campaign had anything to do with WikiLeaks' publications, a U.S. District Court should seriously entertain the idea that the campaign and Stone were Russian cutouts because we say so, and we want this bogus lawsuit to continue. The cost in legal fees alone is a great vengeance against those who refuse to war against Russia. The 14 former Obama intelligence figures signing the brief are led by John Brennan, James Clapper, William J. Burns, Michael V. Hayden, Michael McFaul, and Michael Morell. If I were the judge, I would order up an immediate psychological evaluation of each and every signator.

ZEPP-LAROUCHE WEBCAST

The Coming Collapse of Russia-gate: We Need LaRouche's Four Laws To Move Forward!

This is an edited transcript of Helga Zepp-LaRouche's *weekly webcast of Dec. 14, 2017.*

Harley Schlanger: Hello, I'm Harley Schlanger from the Schiller Institute. Welcome to this week's international strategic briefing from Helga Zepp-LaRouche, the founder and President of the Schiller Institute. I have to say this has been an extraordinary last couple of days, in terms of the unravelling of the so-called Russia-gate investigation, the exposure of the web of corruption surrounding Robert Mueller and his investigation. As we've been saying since the outset of the attacks on Trump, during the campaign last year, this is coming from the highest levels of British intelligence; it includes the networks of Mueller and Comey at the FBI, Justice Department and others. It's quite extraordinary, including the statement from the Deputy Attorney General yesterday in the House Judiciary Committee, when he said it doesn't matter if there's bias, as long as they're able to do their job.

Helga, this is exactly what we pointed out in the special dossier we did on Robert Mueller. Why don't you catch us up on these developments in the last couple of days?

White House/Peter Souza

Robert Mueller

Helga Zepp-LaRouche: This is very fascinating because what is now happening is exactly the opposite of what the intention was: Namely that those people who tried to prove collusion between Trump and the Russian government, are now the targets of a potential investigation themselves, with quite incredible implications. There are already calls out that all of these people—Mueller, McCabe, Bruce Ohr, Peter Strzok, and various other individuals—that they should all be "led away in handcuffs." This is the demand of former judge and prosecutor Jeanine Pirro, on Dec. 9 on Fox Television, and what she referred to is the fact that now it is becoming very clear in the hearings in the House and in the Senate, that there was collusion among people who were clearly a task force against Trump even before he was elected, who wanted to have a sort of "life insurance" policy against the possibility that Trump might be elected, and they worked together with the "former" MI6 agent Christopher Steele on his dirty dossier.

Now, it turns out that the degree of corruption is even much deeper. For example, the wife of the recently demoted Associate Deputy Attorney General Bruce Ohr worked for the very firm which was dealing with Christopher Steele on behalf of the Obama administration and Hillary Clinton election team—namely Fusion GPS.

So there is very clearly conflict of interest, to say the least, and what happened in the hearing was that the situation became so hot that FBI Deputy Director McCabe, at the last moment, "discovered" a so-called conflict in his schedule, and he didn't appear. House Intelligence Chairman Congressman Nunes immediately said that he didn't believe that for a second, because it was not credible. The cover-up no longer works, because the questions asked of these individuals were about things that they should already have volunteered themselves. If there were signs of bias in the investigation, they should have volunteered this themselves without waiting to be asked.

I think this is turning the whole situation around. Russia-gate is crumbling, and this has incredible strategic implications, because this whole thing—if we recall how this developed—was all intended from the very beginning, by the Obama administration, and the leftovers from the previous Bush administration, to prevent President Trump from developing a positive relationship with Russia. And now that it has turned against those who are the accusers, that opens a whole new strategic dimension.

Schlanger: What I'd like to do is go through a couple of the things that came out, including these incredible text messages that were sent from Peter Strzok, who is the former number-two counterintelligence official for the FBI, who was involved in the interrogation of Hillary—I should say the friendly investigation of Hillary Clinton on the emails. He actually softened Comey's conclusions on Hillary Clinton so there would be no legal problem for her. He was involved in the Flynn interview—this guy Strzok is a walking conflict of interest! But the Inspector General of the Justice Department put out 90 pages of SMS messages, and in one of them—this is the one that's most damning—Strzok said to his girlfriend Lisa Page, who is an attorney who worked directly under FBI Deputy Director Andrew

Peter Strzok

McCabe, "I want to believe the path you threw out for consideration in Andy's office, that there's no way Trump gets elected, but I'm afraid we can't take that risk." "Andy" is Andrew McCabe: There was a meeting in McCabe's office to discuss how to keep Trump from getting elected, by top officials of the FBI! I think this is absolutely unprecedented.

Zepp-LaRouche: Yes! It is a coup. And there was a congressman from Florida, Gaetz, who warned Trump that this is a coup against him. I think that that is absolutely the case. President Putin of Russia had said several months ago, that what is going on against Trump is exactly a "Maidan"— I mean the kind of coup which occurred against the Ukrainian government in February 2014. And I think if you look at the *dramatis personae,* the relevant figures, then it's very clear that it is exactly the same apparatus which was also responsible for the Maidan in Kiev. So I think this is not the end of the story, but an incredible crime is just being discovered and being brought into the open.

Schlanger: On the whole question of Mueller and his role, we played a major role in exposing that in our dossier, which we're now going to reprint. People can get that and use it. This is an unfolding story of a coup that we're ahead of! We can cut it off, we can end this attempted coup if we do our job, instead of letting them go ahead unimpeded.

One of the other really striking things in this whole thing is where you see that Fusion GPS and Christopher Steele were brought in by Bruce Ohr, the Associate Deputy Attorney General, for discussion. This shows that the Justice Department and the FBI, back in August of 2016—maybe even in July of 2016—were working out an operation against Trump. Now, is any of this getting out in the media in Europe as far as you know, Helga?

Zepp-LaRouche: No! We are putting it out, but so far, I have not seen any—*any*—coverage of this at all.

U.S. State Department

U.S. Secretary of State Rex Tillerson addressing a press conference, after a UN Security Council meeting on the subject of the Democratic People's Republic of North Korea, Dec. 15, 2017.

What the media are playing up here is the election result in Alabama, as a big blow to Trump—saying that the end of Trump is already in sight. So the picture the European population gets is quite the opposite of what is happening.

Schlanger: The thing that's being kept out of the media because of the focus on all these other kinds of things, is the recent developments around North Korea. Rex Tillerson, the Secretary of State, said that the U.S. is ready for negotiations without preconditions, in cooperation with Russia and China. There have been some other developments around the whole North Korea question. What do you have on that?

Zepp-LaRouche: Somebody in the State Department felt it necessary to immediately correct Tillerson, by saying "yes, that's true,

but now is not the right time." So you can see an ongoing battle on every issue, even in the State Department, with Tillerson being contradicted.

But otherwise, the situation looks hopeful. Certainly the whole North Korean issue is extremely dangerous, because clearly North Korea now is a full-fledged nuclear power; it has ICBMs which can reach everywhere in the United States and many other places as well, and therefore, we are sitting on a powderkeg as long as the U.S. and South Korean, and Japanese military maneuvers are still scheduled.

But there is hope right now, because you had high-level representatives of the United Nations—Under-Secretary-General Feltman, who is an American, and from Russia and China—in Pyongyang. Therefore, if Pyongyang would send a signal that it won't do any tests for the next 60 days, and if the United States calls off this big maneuver which is supposed to start at the beginning of the year, then conditions would be right. Especially if the Tillerson approach of sitting down at the table without preconditions is actually maintained, there is, indeed, hope.

And I think it shows once more, how extremely important it is that the big powers—the United States, Russia, China—work together. Because there are several conflicts in the world which cannot be defused if those powers are on a confrontation course against each other. So I think it is dangerous, but it is also hopeful right now.

Ukraine Narrative Failing

Schlanger: And on this question of the battle against Trump's attempt to bring us into a relationship with China and Russia, we saw two things in the last couple of days: One was Joe Biden's comments against the Russians in Italy. But then, also this crazy speech from National Security Advisor McMaster, who spoke

UN/Rick Bajornas

UN Under-Secretary-General for Political Affairs Jeffrey Feltman, addressing the UN Security Council on Nov. 29, 2017, on the North Korean missile launch.

Ukrainian policeman on fire in Maidan attacks in 2014, during the staged coup which overthrew the government.

at a British-American think tank that's committed to keeping the so-called "special relationship" together, and he said, "geopolitics are back with a vengeance." I think he's answering you on that one, Helga, because you've made the point that we have to get beyond geopolitics. He went on to talk about Russian military "aggression," and Chinese economic aggression. This shows these coup-plotters are still making clear what their intention is.

Zepp-LaRouche: Yes, Biden also claimed that the Russians intervened in the outcome of the referendum concerning the change of the Italian Constitution last year, and he was immediately refuted by the Five-Star party, by the Lega Nord, and by former Prime Minister Berlusconi. Most of the political spectrum in Italy said Biden is completely off.

But I think the truth is about to come out in many places. One other thing on this Russia question is an ongoing trial against the Berkut special police battalion which is standing trial for supposed criminal activity during the Maidan coup in Kiev in early 2014. Now the lawyer for this battalion has two or three witnesses, Georgians, who claim that they had been hired as snipers by Mikheil Saakashvili, from Georgia, at the time; and that they were ordered to shoot on both the demonstrators on the Maidan as well as at the police. And that confirms, again, our analysis of how this thing was completely orchestrated to create chaos and the condition for the coup against Yanukovych.

This is very interesting, because these people will provide testimony in a court case by telephone hookup—obviously, they don't want to appear and admit their deeds, but they are basically admitting what they did—and that means that the whole narrative on Ukraine is also crumbling.

Putin once said that if Ukraine had not happened his opponents, would have invented some other problem, some other story, and I believe that that's true. But as history unfolded, it was Ukraine: first, the $5 billion that Victoria Nuland admitted was spent by the State Department in order to finance the color revolution in Ukraine, starting in 2004—the Orange Revolution and then the Maidan. The whole "narrative" hinges on the fact of the referendum in the Crimea, when the population decided to be part of Russia. And that development was used to demonize Putin, and to impose the sanctions.

However, if you take it back and see that the actual trigger point was not the "annexation" of Crimea, as it is always portrayed, but that there was a staged coup in which snipers fired on people from both sides—that unravels the whole "narrative."

I want to point our readers and viewers to a dossier we published about the Ukraine story as well, because I think "the narrative," as it is called, is failing—you know, narrative means it's not the truth—and I think the truth also has to come out on Ukraine. And then the whole picture—it's almost like a catharsis which is taking place, or we're seeing the beginning of it, but sometimes, such real cleansings are absolutely necessary.

Schlanger: Also the proof that this had nothing to do with the well-being of the people of Ukraine, is the complete dysfunction of the current government, and the fact that Saakashvili, whom you mentioned, led Georgia in a rebellion against Russia and triggered another crisis much earlier. Recently they've been trying to arrest him in Ukraine, and his own organizers have been saying they're going to overthrow the current government of Ukraine!

I would like to call our listeners' attention to a very powerful report given by Natalia Vitrenko, a good friend of yours and the Schiller Institute's, at the recent Schiller Institute conference in Bad Soden. It's available on the New Paradigm Schiller Institute website, http://newparadigm.schillerinstitute.com/media/chinas-initiative-view-ukraine/.

We talked a little bit before about the Italian situation: You mentioned to me before the webcast, a new documentary on the Monte dei Paschi di Siena bank case, and the implications of this for the situation in Europe. What can you tell us about this documentary?

Zepp-LaRouche: I can only advise our viewers to absolutely try to watch this movie. It's a documentary by ARTE, which is the German-French TV channel; it exists so far only in German and in French, but the story told there is absolutely mind-boggling. The title of it is "Death of a Banker," and it refers to the supposed suicide of a banker named David Rossi, on March 6, 2013. He was the communications manager for Monte dei Paschi, the oldest bank in the world. This all occurred in the context of the big financial crisis of 2007-2008, in the circumstances in which a small bank called Antonveneta was taken over by Santander and Monte dei Paschi was drawn into this. There was an incredible amount of wheeling and dealing, covering up losses with derivatives—this looks like another case of Mario Draghi saying he would do whatever it takes to save the euro, which he said as ECB head, in terms of buying up bonds and quantitative easing. However, this is a case where that question comes up. Because it was Draghi in his function as head of the Banca d'Italia, who agreed to this wheeling and dealing, even if much was completely dubious.

Now clearly this David Rossi knew about criminal activities inside and outside of the bank. The thing that makes this documentary so absolutely suspenseful, is video footage which shows the end-phase of his fall from his office building, and then shows him lying dead on the street. Then a man, another banker from the same bank, comes by without even looking closely or trying to help him, walks away, comes back, and makes a call on his mobile phone—this is all very, very suspicious.

There is now a new forensic investigation in Italy into the circumstances of this supposed suicide. The initial findings say that he could not have fallen by himself, and end up in the position in which he landed on the street. His wife is very active, and his family does not believe it was suicide at all; she has already posted this movie on her Facebook page, even though it's only in German and French so far—and it's going viral. The mainstream media are not yet reporting it, but this is an unbelievable story.

One implication is that a banker from Deutsche Bank who was also found dead in London one year later [in January 2014], a person called William Broeksmit, was involved in similar financial arrangements.

This is a case where it has been said that the Italian banking crisis created a risk to the European system, but as the authors of this movie have pointed out, the Italian banking system was completely fine, including Monte dei Paschi, until Italy was forced to have a huge privatization of its banking sector to supposedly make Italy ripe for the euro.

I would guess that this is not the end of it, because there are now criminal investigations into the circumstances, and this is clearly another case where you see the criminal activity around this banking system. I think our viewers should really watch this movie.

European Union Flounders

Schlanger: This just underscores the whole point that what's going on in Italy, and what's going on with the investigation into the Maidan, exposes how the total instability of Europe is part of the reason for the coup against Trump: Because beginning with the Brexit, we have been seeing the disintegration of political parties in Europe, and the loss of any approach to a real production policy. We see the Chinese becoming very much involved in Europe right now.

And I'd like you to give us a quick update on what's going on in Germany: Because it appears as though there's still a very significant problem in putting together a new government after the recent elections.

Zepp-LaRouche: Well, it's now already two and half months since the elections, and the first effort by Merkel to form a government with the [Free Democratic] liberal party and the Greens failed. Now, they're trying again, a Grand Coalition with the Social Democrats (SPD), but in the Social Democracy there is a lot of opposition against the continuation of the policy which almost destroyed the SPD in the earlier coalition. The crazy proposal by Martin Schulz, the head of the SPD, is now to form another Grand Coalition, but this time it will be a "cooperation coalition," which is the idea that they only agree on certain particular points, and then place ministers into the cabinet on that basis; and on the points they don't agree on, each side can be free to form opposition coalitions in the Bundestag, in the parlia-

German Chancellor Angela Merkel addressing Parliament, April 29, 2017.

ment—which obviously is ridiculous. Because how can you be in the government and oppose your own government at the same time? And that would also mean that on certain issues, the CDU/CSU could only get a majority by relying on the AfD, the Alternative for Germany, which is an extreme right-wing party which has very dangerous elements within it.

So I think this is total instability. As long as you don't have a government in Germany, all the plans for Europe are null and void, because without a German government those plans cannot be implemented.

What is on the table right now are various proposals which only differ in nuances: One is by French President Macron, which is to have a European Finance Minister, and a European budget. Then you have [EU Commission] President Juncker, who wants to put everything under the European Union Commission, and build that bureaucracy up as a European government; and German SPD leader Martin Schulz, who says, "yes, we must have a United States of Europe."

This is a very absurd proposal; it was absurd all along, because there is no European people. There are many different cultures, traditions, and languages— and people in one part of Europe have no inkling what's going on in another part of Europe because they can't read the newspapers, they don't understand the history, and they are totally uninformed—so there's no European people.

But if this scheme was already dubious many years ago, it is completely impossible now, because the East Europeans, the Central Europeans, and people from the Balkans have a completely different attitude towards China's New Silk Road. There is Austria, where the new coalition government program even includes a paragraph that Austria will cooperate with the Belt and Road Initiative. Switzerland is excited to be cooperating with China in this respect. Hungary just now blocked a NATO/Ukraine commission meeting, because they don't agree with the policy of NATO encircling Russia. And so there is no unity. But clearly, this is all because they don't want to look at the axioms of their policy failures.

In the rest of the world, there is a growing awareness that Europe is not functioning, but I think it requires a real policy discussion: What are the principles of economy? What is in the interest of the people? How should we form a policy, a vision for the future? And none of these things has been addressed by the present coalition discussions in Germany.

But there is a growing demand, coming from industry, from the Mittelstand [small and medium-sized industry, especially high technology]—and the Schiller Institute is holding events to try to make the policy of the Silk Road better known. People must know more about the real advantages of cooperating with the Belt and Road Initiative—for example, in the reconstruction of Syria which is now seriously on the table, especially because of the roles of Russia and China; and also the need to cooperate in the development of Africa. The problem is, rather than joining hands in win-win cooperation with China, what Brussels—and unfortunately also Berlin—are saying, is they feel that they have to be in geopolitical competition with China.

And I think this problem of thinking in geopolitical terms is the main obstacle. If you look at the long arc of human history, it is very clear that unless we develop a vision of one, single, humanity working towards the common aims of mankind, we are not going to make it, and we will always be in danger of war. In the time of thermonuclear weapons, this could be fatal for the human race.

So we have to develop a different perspective on how nations can cooperate.

Schlanger: I think we have a perfect example of that coming from China right now. There's a discussion about investment in providing electricity for more than one billion people in mostly Africa and South Asia. The

President Trump signing Space Directive 1 on Dec. 11, 2017, to relaunch the U.S. space program.

Chinese are talking about $1.5 trillion investment to do that! That's obviously aimed at precisely what you're talking about—the improvement of the future for people who otherwise have no hope.

I'd like to come back to one final point here, which again, gets at this question of why they're trying to get rid of Trump. There was an announcement a couple of days ago by President Trump about the U.S. space program, and his commitment to take the United States back to the Moon, and beyond to Mars and to other planets, other galaxies, even. This kind of optimism was also seen in a China-U.S. conference on space, where there was discussion about collaboration for the future—which by the way, right now is not allowed, because of the rules against the U.S. scientists talking to the Chinese, enforced by the same FBI that we've seen in this conflict of interest.

So, what are your thoughts on this great potential for the space cooperation?

Zepp-LaRouche: There is also an agreement between the United States and Russia to build a lunar space station together, a decision by Trump—you can really see who is who when you see how people react to that. ESA, the European Space Agency, was completely enthusiastic and welcomed that; the Chinese government expressed happiness about this decision. The European media covered it as though Trump were completely crazy to go back to the Moon—this is really incredible! The people who have been in space, the astronauts, come back and say, "this is an incredible experience, because in space, it doesn't matter what nationality you are, because you have to rely on each other, otherwise you can't carry our such an extremely challenging mission." And a Russian cosmonaut just said: We should develop an attitude of solving problems on Earth with the same spirit with which we cooperate in space.

That is a point we have been making for a very long time, that once you take the view that man is not an Earth-bound earthling, but that we are continuing the process of evolution, not only by developing infrastructure across all continents, and developing a World Land-Bridge—but that the next natural step in infrastructure development is in nearby space. Industrializing the Moon is the precondition for longer space-flights to other planets; and that is the natural identity of man, that we are part of that universe, and not just earthlings with limited resources.

So I think it's a very optimistic thing that President Trump has reconnected to the spirit of John F. Kennedy. This is exactly what we have been fighting for, to put an end to the negative cultural paradigm of the period between John F. Kennedy's assassination and the end of the Obama administration when space was really on the back burner, and no fundamental progress was made.

I think this is all reason for optimism, and you should really help to get this message out, because the mass media are keeping the lid on a lot of positive developments which would give people enormous optimism if only they knew about them.

Schlanger: And to close with that thought, we are now releasing a new pamphlet titled, "America's Future on the New Silk Road," which outlines why, as you said, this is not just necessary, but how Lyndon LaRouche, your husband, developed the economic policy, his Four Laws, on how we can do it. Without those four basic laws, we're not going to be able to take advantage of this, and that's a central part of this fight.

So Helga, this has been a very rapidly moving discussion today. I thank you for giving us this update, and I'm sure that events are going to continue at this accelerating pace. We'll be back again next week, with the next Schiller Institute international webcast. Thank you.

Zepp-LaRouche: Bye-bye.

Targeting Poverty
In China and Italy

by Michele Geraci

The following is an edited transcript of the November 21, 2017 videocast lecture by Michele Geraci, a China-based professor and think tank expert on international economics and the Chinese economy. It is Part 8 of the videocast, "China Economy and Society," available on YouTube at https://youtu.be/pXglcE_nqvE and his web-site.

China is very proud of its great success in poverty reduction, now having only 45 million people living below the poverty line, which is one dollar per day, or equivalent to about $360 per year. That represents about 3% of the population of China; only 3% of the people are now living in extreme poverty.

Even more important, however, is that China now has a goal, that by 2020—in the next three years—the number of people in extreme poverty will be zero; there will be a total eradication of poverty. From 1978 to today, 850 million people have been lifted out of poverty. How has China done this? It has a plan, as it does in everything; China has a plan, a targeted poverty reduction plan that can be outlined in six points. The first point is that China has a mapping of who these 45 million people are, where they live, and has identified twelve areas, twelve counties around China where these 45 million people live. These areas include Tibet, some southwestern counties and southwestern provinces,

and some in the northeast and the north of China. We can outline this Chinese plan in the following six points:

1. Knowing who those people are, knowing where live. It's like keeping a record. Every poor person has a card; we know who they are, where they live, how much money they make. We know who they are.
2. The plan maps out the government officials responsible for those areas, whether it be on the county level or the head of a small village, or political cadre—we know the names of the people who are responsible in these areas where the 45 million poor people reside.
3. China has decided, depending on where these people live and what they do, that for each of them there

Michele Geraci, shown in a video presentation demonstrating mapping of areas for poverty reduction in China.

Michele Geraci

must be a plan or a program of poverty alleviation. This could be training or micro-credit loans—micro-financing has done a lot—or it could be plans including food programs, housing programs—prime necessities.

4. Building infrastructure. After having identified where these people live, China will decide what roads to build, sanitation systems, water, irrigation, and even—to make this poverty eradication sustainable—developing agri-business and tourism in rural areas.

5. The creation and reinforcement of social groups in these localized areas are very important. Those people who are not in dire need of the help from the government make their own time available, their own resources available to help the community. That creates an important sense of community. So it is not merely individuals for whom poverty is eradicated, but a success which becomes a success for the small village, of the county area.

6. The "performance review" is an important, critical element in making the previous steps work. Every government official at the end of the year advances in his political career according to whether or not he has met this poverty reduction target.

So what do we have here? We have a very well thought-out plan that goes from the top down, with central government directives to eradicate poverty, bring-ing this number to zero in three years' time, and at the same time, cascading responsibility down to the local officials in order to make sure that the implementation is done correctly; the rewards system rewards those that succeed. So there is a complete alignment of interest from top to bottom, and this is the reason why China succeeds in doing things.

The Comparison with Italy

Compare this success to the rate of poverty in Italy. While the number of people living below the poverty line in China is 3%, in our country, in Italy, we have five million people living below the poverty line, which is about 8% of the population. Now, of course, we cannot immediately compare 3% with the Italian 8% because the definition of poverty in China is about $360 per year; in Italy it is about 600 euros per month for a single household, or about 1,000 euros per month for households composed of three people, which is equivalent to about 300 euros per person per month of income.

We are looking at almost ten times higher. But, taking into account the cost of living, we do have a serious problem in Italy. Of course the 5 million people do not live in a situation of extreme poverty like the 45 million people in China, but China is still very proud of this 3% result. Perhaps once again, we in Italy and in other western countries should look at China and implement a program which has similar characteristics. What I must emphasize is that things get done only when there is total alignment of interest, when the central government policy is implemented by people at the bottom—people who will wake up in the morning, and before opening their eyes they think, how will I get the poverty number down to zero? Without that, we talk and we don't do anything.

Geraci is an Adjunct Professor of Finance at NYU (New York University) Shanghai, the first Sino-U.S. joint venture university approved by the Ministry of Education of the People's Republic of China, which started in 2013. He is also the Head of the China Economic Policy Program at Nottingham University Business School, and Senior Research Fellow and Adjunct Professor of Finance at Zhejiang University. He holds an MBA from the M.I.T. Sloan School of Management and a Masters in Electronic Engineering from the University of Palermo, Italy.

'Death of a Banker' Spotlights Draghi and The Dying, Criminal Financial System

by Emidio Castellani

Dec. 17—In 2012, "Whatever it takes" was the famous statement with which current European Central Bank (ECB) President Mario Draghi made it clear that the Eurosystem was ready to walk over corpses in order to save the euro-denominated financial bubble and its banking system. The sinister implications of that statement resonate when you watch the documentary film "Death of a Banker: Scandal over the World's Oldest Bank" (*Tod eines Bankers: Der Skandal um die älteste Bank der Welt*). The 55-minute film was broadcast by the French-German TV channel ARTE on Dec. 12, 2017. Here we have a real corpse: David Rossi, head of communications of Monte dei Paschi di Siena (MPS) bank until March 6, 2013, the day when he fell from his office window in an alleged suicide.

Although David Rossi's mysterious "suicide" is now an active case in Italy, and the Siena prosecution has recently re-opened the investigation of his death, Moritz Enders' ARTE documentary film has the merit of bringing that so-called suicide and its larger implications to an international audience. Not only that: "Death of a Banker" brings to light the international dimension of what mainstream media and economists call "the Italian banking crisis," of which MPS is the pivot. Far from being a local or national issue, the MPS crisis was created by decisions taken in the 2008 global bank bailout by central bankers and supervisors—the same central bankers who today are blaming Italian banks for being mismanaged!

The film reconstructs the dynamics of Rossi's fall from the window of his MPS office, with the help of forensic experts and witnesses, and concludes that Rossi could not have done it alone. The reasons why Rossi might have been "suicided" are spelled out clearly: He knew about criminal actions involving very high-level people, inside and outside the bank.

David Rossi's was not the only mysterious death in the MPS case. Less than a year after his death, on Jan. 26, 2014, banker Will Broeksmit was found hanging from a dog leash in his London Apartment—reported as a suicide. Broeksmit had been the head of Capital and Risk Optimization for Deutsche Bank until February 2013, and had worked at the bank until his 2014 death. Broeksmit had been involved in the sale of the derivative instruments to MPS that have been the subject of criminal investigations in Italy. A third banker, Calogero "Charlie" Gambino, was found hanging from an upstairs balcony in his Brooklyn home three months later. Gambino had been a regulatory lawyer for Deutsche Bank for 11 years.

Screenshot of the the documentary, "Death of a Banker."

Headquarters of the Italian bank, Monte dei Paschi di Siena.

The MPS trail leads to the City of London and Wall Street. One thread connects the three murder victims: They all knew about fraudulent derivative deals between Deutsche Bank and MPS, aimed at cooking the MPS books and covering losses, and they all were soon to be called as witnesses in official investigations.

Cooking the Books

Three key elements of the MPS crisis are treated in the documentary: The bizarre acquisition of Banca Antonveneta from Santander in 2008, the derivative contracts to cover the losses, and the large loans to political friends, which then turned into non-performing loans (NPLs).

From 2008 to 2016, the equity capital of MPS had lost over 90% of its value, going from 5.7 billion euro to half a billion, despite two capital increases, a government bailout, and a partial bail-in. With over 45 billion euro in NPLs, MPS was facing insolvency. Finally, in 2017, in order to avoid insolvency, the Italian government carried out a "pre-emptive recapitalization," which was a *de facto* nationalization.

The shocked citizens of the Italian city of Siena asked, "What happened? How could the oldest bank in the world, Monte dei Paschi di Siena, founded in 1472, have been so mismanaged to create such a disaster?" Almost every family in Siena is a shareholder and many of them had lost all their savings.

The turning point was the acquisition of the Italian bank Antonveneta from Santander in 2008. Documents show that Mario Draghi, then Governor of the Bank of Italy, ignored his own supervisors in allowing the MPS purchase of Antonveneta and misrepresented the real cost of the operation. In the documentary, Paolo Emilio Falaschi, attorney for MPS' small shareholders, shows the Draghi letter in which he authorized the purchase, presenting a total "cost" of 9 billion euro—but that was the price, not the cost. Falaschi explains that the total cost, which included Antonveneta's liabilities, was over 17 billion euro.

In an attempt to paper over the losses produced by the real cost, MPS fraudulently altered its books through derivative contracts, such as one sold by Deutsche Bank, called "Project Santorini." The deal appeared on the books as an asset, whereas it was actually a loss shifted to the future. However, normal supervision would have immediately uncovered the fraud.

Financial expert Giuseppe Bivona, a consultant to the Inquiry Commission of the Tuscany Regional Council that issued a report on the MPS crisis in July 2016, says in the documentary: "If in the contract, the word 'derivative' pops up 447 times, it is not difficult to understand that this is not about government bonds ... From 2010 to 2015, the bank engaged systematically in cooking its books, by the admission of its own managers."

Indeed, a trial in Milan has recently exposed the fact that the Bank of Italy at that time was aware of the fact that such derivatives were created to cook the books of MPS, in order to cover half a billion euro losses. Former senator Elio Lannutti, head of the Italian consumer association Adusbef, says in the documentary that Mario Draghi is responsible for "criminal activity."

Privatization, Deregulation

The final blow to MPS was delivered by the economic recession primarily caused by the austerity programs implemented by the Mario Monti government in

2011. Monti was appointed prime minister under a conspiracy "led by Brussels, Frankfurt, and the Quirinale in Rome," according to the then Finance Minister Giulio Tremonti—meaning the European Union (EU) Commission, the ECB, and the Italian State Presidency under Giorgio Napolitano. Tremonti's government, led by Prime Minister Silvio Berlusconi, was given an ultimatum through a letter written by the outgoing and the incoming heads of the ECB, Jean-Claude Trichet and Mario Draghi, who stated that the ECB would stop supporting Italian debt paper—unless the government implemented "reforms" including a change in the constitution, labor reforms, brutal budget cuts, and tax increases.

Facing ECB retaliation, the Berlusconi cabinet resigned in November 2011. The technocratic government led by Mario Monti executed the ECB orders, plunging the country into a recession. As a consequence of a wave of corporate and household insolvencies, NPLs mushroomed in the Italian banking system. Today, MPS has a backlog of over 45 billion in NPLs; the entire Italian banking system is estimated to hold one third of the total one trillion euro of NPLs in the Eurozone.

Meanwhile, banking supervision has been centralized in the EU under the European Banking Authority, which is a branch of the ECB. The ECB is exclusively focusing on the Italian NPL crisis and demanding action to defuse what it claims is the unique systemic risk to the European and global financial system. Mainstream economists and media have made the Italian problem a totem, while ignoring the much bigger risk posed by the derivatives exposure of German, French, and British banks.

EU rules have made it impossible for banks to find solutions, by imposing rules that prohibit further loans to defaulting customers. Banks are thus prevented from any negotiated solutions with their customers. Bridge loans, for a certain period, would allow business customers to keep going, and be in a position to repay their loans, or allow individuals to have some breathing room while finding a new job. On top of that, the ECB is now considering a new rule by which banks would have to put up a 100% reserve for NPLs.

While doing this, the ECB has also issued a deadline for banks to get rid of their NPLs, forcing them to sell the loans to hedge funds which buy them for ten cents on the dollar and make up to 400% profit on the collat-

© European Union 2017

European Central Bank (ECB) President Mario Draghi.

sion under Jacques Delors, which mandated all member states to lift national regulations and bank separation provisions, in favor of a "single banking model" in the EU—universal banks. The directive listed all permissible activities under the new banking model, including investing in a detailed list of derivative products.

Why Was MPS Sacrificed?

That directive was implemented in Italy by two figures—Mario Draghi, then director-general of the Italian Treasury, and Giuliano Amato, prime minister in 1992-1993 and 2000-2001. After participating in the famous meeting on board the Queen's yacht *Britannia* with City of London bankers on June 2, 1992, Draghi was appointed head of the Privatizations Committee, which oversaw all Italian privatizations, starting with banks, including MPS. At the same time, Draghi and Amato drafted the two bills that deregulated the banking system and lifted banking separation rules, called "the Amato-Draghi Bill" or the Single Banking Act of 1995.

Draghi eventually left the Treasury in 2002 and became head of European operations at Goldman Sachs in London. In 2006, he became Governor of the Bank of Italy after his predecessor, Antonio Fazio, had been overthrown by the scandal around Antonveneta bank. Fazio had opposed the sale of Antonveneta to ABN Amro, but had to resign when the media published wiretapped conversations between Fazio and the Italian rivals of ABN in the purchase.

Giuliano Amato, between his two mandates as Italian prime minister, was hired by the EU Commission to draft what became the Lisbon Treaty in 2006. After the original "European Constitution" text was rejected by referenda in France and Holland, Amato was assigned to change the text a little in order to reintroduce it in form of a treaty. That treaty is today the primary source for European Law.

A member of the British Fabian Society, Amato has been the *deus ex machina* of MPS, together with his ally Franco Bassanini, a former minister and a member of parliament from Siena. Amato and Bassanini have been the sponsors of Giuseppe Mussari, the CEO of MPS, who launched the Antonveneta operation and the subsequent derivative orgy. (Mussari left MPS in 2010 and became head of the Italian Banking Association until his resignation in January 2013.) See "A Four-Century-Old Nemesis Casts Its Shadow over Upcoming Elections" in *EIR*, February 1, 2013, for more background.

This is a closed circle: It is hard to imagine that MPS CEO Mussari, a lawyer by profession, decided, by himself, to buy Antonveneta in 2008 with nothing but a phone call to Santander's head Emilio Botin—without due diligence—while knowing that the price was overblown. It is easy to imagine that Mussari was told to do so by someone who had enough power to guarantee that things would eventually be smoothed over and fixed, and that he would be protected. Mussari's protector Amato fits the description. But what was the higher reason for deliberately exposing MPS to bankruptcy? What was a reason strong enough to consider the oldest bank in the world "expendable"?

Mario Draghi could answer that question. At the time of the Antonveneta takeover, Draghi was not only the head of Italy's central bank, but also head of the Bank for International Settlements connected Financial Stability Forum, a body created in 1999 to suggest proposals to "reform" the financial system in the wake of the 1997-98 collapse, but also to take action in case of a crisis. In 2008, the world financial system was on the verge of collapse. Governments throughout the world were handing out trillions of dollars and euros to bail out insolvent megabanks.

When ABN Amro became insolvent and a chain-reaction was threatened, it was bailed out by a consortium of banks in what was the largest European insolvency of all time, with over 60 billion euro. The consortium was composed of the Royal Bank of Scotland, the Belgian Fortis, and the Spanish Banco Santander. They chopped up ABN Amro and took over its parts—Santander got Antonveneta. However, as a result, Santander found itself in trouble and announced a capital increase of ten billion euro in order to offset the losses.

Was MPS sacrificed to bail out Santander? Was Draghi's fraudulent authorization motivated by the higher purposes of saving the global financial system "whatever it takes"? It is a fact that the sale of Antonveneta brought 17 billions into Santander's vault and the capital increase was cancelled.

Plan B for the Next Crisis?

The rest is known. Members of the Investigating Committee on the Banking Crisis of the Italian Parliament, which has discussed the MPS case, have asked Draghi to testify before the committee. The ECB made known that the head of the ECB is not accountable to any national parliament. This makes it even more urgent to replace so-called "EU Law" and the EU institutional framework with a system of cooperation among sovereign nations allowing nations to re-establish banking separation systems, among other regulations.

Such an urgent banking reform was an issue during the discussion with a selected audience of journalists and bankers at the showing of the documentary in Berlin. The former head of the Association of Public Banks in Germany, Bernd Lüthje, called for separating "normal" banks from investment banks. Normal banks, he said, which manage savings and deposits, should not be allowed to speculate. On the other side, investment banks should be "strictly controlled."

In his interview with DWN, filmmaker Moritz Enders describes the dead end which the euro system is in now and said, "I really hope that in the [German] Finance Ministry they have a Plan B for the next euro crisis. In an uncertain situation, a controlled demolition is better than an uncontrolled collapse, which could be provoked by an Italian exit. I believe that this issue is of fundamental importance for the EU. And I believe that our film on the Monte dei Paschi helps a bit in the necessary debate."

Every Day Counts In Today's Showdown To Save Civilization

Trump's Space Directive: Back to the Moon with a Renewed Purpose?

by Kesha Rogers, independent candidate for Congress from the Texas 9th CD

Dec. 18 (EIRNS)—Space Policy Directive 1, signed by President Trump on Dec. 11, represents a change in our national space policy, to return human beings to the Moon and then carry out a mission to Mars and beyond. In his address during the signing ceremony, the President declared,

> The directive I'm signing today will refocus America's space program on Human exploration and discovery. It marks an important step in returning American Astronauts to the Moon for the first time since 1972 for long term exploration and use. This time we will not only plant our flag and leave our footprint. We will establish a foundation for an eventual mission to Mars, and perhaps someday to many worlds beyond. This directive will ensure America's space program, once again, leads and inspires all of humanity.

The signing of this directive came only nine months after the President signed the NASA Transition Authorization Act of 2017, in March. Shortly after that, the President relaunched the National Space Council, with Vice President Pence at its head. The first meeting of the council, on October 5, unanimously recommended a plan to return human beings to the lunar surface.

This year marks the 45th anniversary of the Apollo 17 Moon landing on December 7, 1972, the last time that human beings walked on the surface of the Moon. Apollo astronaut. Harrison Schmitt, the last living crew member of that Apollo 17 mission, was present at the signing of

NASA

Harrison Schmitt on the Moon, Dec. 11, 1972.

the space policy directive on Dec. 11. He has not only advocated a national mission to return to the lunar surface, but has been a strong proponent of mining helium-3 on the Moon for advanced propulsion and other energy uses.

During the ceremony, the President pledged that we will return to the Moon. Addressing Schmitt, he said,

> Exactly forty-five years ago, almost to the minute, Jack became the last American to land on the Moon. Today we pledge that he will not be the last, and I suspect that we will be finding other places to land, in addition to the Moon.

This new policy under President Trump shuts down the ridiculous plan of sending human beings to an asteroid, and commits the USA to making lunar exploration a national priority.

In 2010 this author launched her campaign as a candidate for the U.S. House of Representatives, to save our national space program from the hideous and destructive cuts of former president Obama, who declared, in reference to the need to send human beings back to the lunar surface, that we had "been there, done that." President Obama's policy did not merely reject the relaunching of a lunar mission; he rejected the future progress that a full lunar development mission—requiring and enabling the breakthrough to thermonuclear fusion power—would mean for humanity as a whole. Obama condemned the very idea of the quality of national mission that would restore optimism to the country and unify it around a real science driver and economic recovery program, as expressed in a national space mission coherent with Krafft Ehricke's Three Laws of Astronautics (see box).

A national space mission renews the opportunity to launch a real physical economic recovery program for the nation. Such a real recovery program requires the adoption of Lyndon LaRouche's four economic laws to save the United States—specifically, abandoning the use of Wall Street to generate profits from speculation, and employing a federal credit system, through which credit is issued to—

generate high productivity trends in improvement of employment, with the accompanying intention, to increase the physical-economic productivity, and living standards of the persons and households of the United States.

Examples include upgrading to high-speed rail for freight and passenger transportation, upgrading to nuclear fission and fusion for abundant electrical power, and upgrading to a full human space program that brings our Moon into the economic grasp of mankind, garnering all the spin-off technologies of all of these upgrades to every sector of our economy, including agriculture, medicine, machine tool design, and supply-chain logistics.

In essence, this requires a crash science-driver program to develop a fusion energy economy, and the exploration and development of space, which is also key to the productive cultural and economic future of our nation, and the world.

Remember the unifying words of President John F. Kennedy:

For the eyes of the world now look into space, to the Moon and to the planets beyond, and we have vowed that we shall not see it governed by a hostile flag of conquest, but by a banner of freedom and peace. We have vowed that we shall not see space filled with weapons of mass destruction, but with instruments of knowledge and understanding.

The instruments of knowledge and understanding must be our renewed commitment today to peaceful cooperation in the development and exploration of space with all nations. We must abolish any laws that prevent our national space agency from working in cooperation with any nation, including China. China has taken a leading role in space exploration through its national space program, and responded very positively to the announced plans of the United States to send human beings back to the surface of the Moon and on to Mars. In a press briefing, China Foreign Ministry spokesperson Lu Kang said, "China is glad to see countries making progress in the exploration and use of outer space for peaceful purposes." He said, "China hopes members of the international community will reach an agreement on preventing the weaponization of outer space."

It is time for President Trump to commit our nation to join with all leading nations of the world in a community of shared destiny in the exploration and development of space, as the basis for meeting the challenges and solving problems facing all mankind.

The President of the United States will address the nation on January 30 in his first State of the Union Address. We must see to it that nothing gets in the way of him fulfilling a commitment to renew our national mission and restore optimism to our nation.

Krafft Ehricke's 'Three Laws'

Ehricke summarized his philosophy of astronautics in three laws (1957):

First Law. Nobody and nothing under the natural laws of this universe impose any limitations on man except man himself.

Second Law. Not only the Earth, but the entire Solar System, and as much of the universe as he can reach under the laws of nature, are man's rightful field of activity.

Third Law. By expanding through the universe, man fulfills his destiny as an element of life, endowed with the power of reason and the wisdom of the moral law within himself.

The first law is astronautics' challenge to man to write his declaration of independence from *a priori* thinking, from uncritically accepted conditions, in other words, from a past and principally different pre-technological world clinging to him. This can be done.

The Declaration of Independence and the Constitution of this country prove it.

—Cited in *Krafft Ehricke's Extraterrestrial Imperative* by Marsha Freeman (Apogee Books, 2009).

What Will It Take
To Go Back to the Moon?

by Marsha Freeman, *EIR* Technology Editor

Dec. 17—President Trump has put a vision for the future of space exploration before the American public, which would reignite the optimism and scientific accomplishments of the 1960s Apollo Program. The Space Policy Directive 1 that the President signed at the White House on December 11 pledges that "America will lead in space again." The new space policy commits the United States to return to the Moon, overturning eight years of the Obama Administration's sabotage of that critical next step in space exploration.

"The directive I am signing today will refocus America's space program on human exploration and discovery," said the President. "It marks an important step in returning American astronauts to the Moon for the first time since 1972,

President Trump signing Space Policy Directive 1.

NASA/Aubrey Gemignani

for long-term exploration and use. This time we will not only plant our flag and leave our footprint, we will establish a foundation for an eventual mission to Mars and perhaps, some day, to many worlds beyond."

At the ceremony, the President was flanked by two current astronauts, and three former astronauts, including Harrison (Jack) Schmitt. Schmitt was on the Apollo 17 mission 45 years ago, which was the last to land astronauts on the Moon. Recognizing the occasion of the anniversary, President Trump turned to Schmitt. "Exactly 45 years ago, almost to the minute, Jack became one of the last Americans to land on the Moon," said the President. "Today we pledge that he will not be the last, and I suspect that we will be finding other places to land in addition to the Moon."

NASA's leadership not-so-subtly made its preference clear, by bringing a piece of Moon rock to the White House ceremony, which had been collected by Harrison Schmitt during the Apollo 17 mission, "as a reminder of exploration history."

"This directive will ensure America's space pro-

gram once again leads and inspires all of humanity," the President said. We will "lift our eyes all the way up to the heavens."

"Imagine the possibility waiting in those big beautiful stars if we dare to dream big. That's what our country is doing again, we're dreaming big."

The goal of the nation's space program, to move human civilization beyond Earth to the Moon, was to be the next step after Apollo. The outline of that mission was based on the decades of planning by a group of German space pioneers who came to the United States with the specific goal of mankind's exploration and development of the Moon. One of these, the visionary Krafft Ehricke, who determined that space exploration is not an option, but an "extraterrestrial imperative," had, by 1970, created a detailed road map for the scientific and industrial development of the Moon.

Lyndon LaRouche brought the necessity of a "crash program" for space exploration into the national spotlight in January 1987, during his presidential campaign, with his nationally televised broadcast titled, "The

Woman on Mars." LaRouche envisioned a colony on Mars to be operational within 40 years, built on the foundation of the previous decades' industrial development of the Moon. He describes not only the technological breakthroughs that would make Moon and Mars colonization possible, but the cultural paradigm shift that would bring Americans, and particularly our youth, back to a science-centered world view, and an optimism about the future.

Now decades later, after previous false starts, there is the opportunity to revive the "spirit of Apollo." But to bring the lunar return that President Trump supports to reality, along with his other objectives, such as his multi-trillion-dollar infrastructure plan, will require a complete reconceptualization of the economy and economic policy. Lyndon LaRouche's Four Laws provide us with the conceptual framework. An economy vectored toward a credit system that energizes investment in science, technology, revolutionary advances in industry, and the general welfare of the population, will lay the basis for the President's vision.

President Kennedy's Apollo program succeeded because he took personal responsibility to organize political support for it as a national mission, and because his FDR-inspired economic priorities included upgrades in education and healthcare, an investment tax credit to encourage industry to expand and modernize, federal investments in infrastructure, and an R&D tax credit, to create new technologies to up-shift the productivity of the economy as a whole.

Twice since President Kennedy's Apollo program, there have been announcements of Moon/Mars missions for NASA. But neither that of President George H.W. Bush nor George W. Bush came to fruition. President Trump has the opportunity now to put the U.S. on the path to realize what space visionaries have long prepared: to make mankind a space-faring species.

Industrial Development of the Moon

Living on the Moon, and creating an industrial economy and science hub there, will require what development projects on Earth require—infrastructure.

Krafft Ehricke's concept of a lunar program was that the economy of the Moon, seen as our planet's seventh continent, should be integrated with that of the Earth. This would create an "open world" for Earth, burying once and for all the fallacy that there are "limits to growth." The mineral and metals resources of the Moon, the manufactured products produced from them, and the cache of unique resources such as helium-3,

Krafft Ehricke (1917-1984)

would supplement those on Earth. Fission, and later, fusion energy would provide the large-scale power sources for lunar industry and the city on the Moon. Astronomical observatories, particularly on the far side of the Moon, undisturbed by electromagnetic noise from Earth, would open a new window to the Universe. A new civilization would be created of citizens who call the Moon, not the Earth, "home."

To get from here to there, the first step is for a robust infrastructure in Earth orbit, as Ehricke proposed. Unmanned spacecraft for all of the applications we have today would be upgraded, including telecommunications, Earth remote sensing, and weather forecasting, as well as arrays of scientific satellites for Earth and space studies.

A "space station," with functions greatly expanded from those of today's International Space Station, would be a city in space, which Ehricke descriptively called "Astropolis." Specialists would check out and then launch spacecraft to Mars, and activities that benefit from microgravity, such as medical treatment, would be offered in the city. Visitors would share the experience previously only available to astronauts, of seeing the Earth from space as the home of mankind.

A fleet of nuclear-powered cargo vehicles, which Ehricke called the Diana fleet, would shuttle between Earth orbit and lunar orbit. The cargo vehicles would deliver supplies from Earth to the Moon to build and supply industry and the lunar city, and would return to Earth orbit with raw materials and, increasingly, with manufactured products from the Moon.

The colonists on the Moon would not live in "habitats," or a lunar "base," but in Selenopolis, a city with thousands of residents. With time, Selenopolis would

Chris Sloan

Selenopolis, as envisioned by Krafft Ehricke, is not a habitat or lunar "base," but a city on the Moon.

become economically self-sufficient and create the platform from which to continue on to Mars.

While Krafft Ehricke's magnificent multi-decade plan for the settlement and industrialization of the Moon is not yet on the table, President Trump's new space policy creates the possibility to take the steps necessary to fulfill it, since the President has directed that America's return of humans to the Moon will be for "long-term exploration and utilization."

The Return to the Moon

NASA has been anticipating that the new leadership in the White House would reverse the lunar ban of the Obama Administration. A small lunar technology development effort had continued, and the leadership of the space agency has stated that development of the lunar-landing Altair spacecraft that was halted under the Obama Administration, could be quickly restarted.

In order to prepare for what was hoped would be the Trump Administration's return to the Moon, NASA has designed a Deep Space Gateway, a small-scale lunar orbital facility to be manned periodically, with no landings included. This bare-bones, almost half-hearted design, pales in comparison to the accomplishments of the Apollo program and to President Trump's directive.

But even this minimal concept has generated support from Russia, Japan, and Europe, who are no doubt relieved that sanity has returned to the U.S. space program.

The head of the European Space Agency (ESA), Jan Woerner, has put forward the idea of a Moon Village. This is a general concept he makes clear, which envisions a multitude of separate components and facilities on the Moon, contributed by governments, private companies, and any other parties with the capability.

Among the current programs for unmanned, robotic exploration, South Korea is developing the technology for a Pathfinder lunar orbiter mission, and later lunar lander. India is preparing its Chandrayaan-2 lunar mission for launch, to include an orbiter, lander, and rover, to follow its highly successful first orbital Moon mission. Japan also plans a follow-on to its Selene orbital mission, to also include a lander and rover.

China is pursuing a long-term, methodical lunar exploration program, which will undoubtedly culminate in a manned presence on the Moon. Each mission is extending China's capabilities for exploration and for breaking new ground in science and engineering. Long-term lunar exploration goals have frequently been stated, and include the mining of helium-3 from soil on the lunar surface as a fuel for fusion power plants. It is that ability, to plan decades ahead in order to fulfill a national mission, that distinguishes the Chinese program from the others now underway.

China's space exploration program is not a stand-alone project, but a centerpiece of its goal of creating a "knowledge-based society" that drives economic growth and creates the scientific talent to make the breakthroughs of the future.

The United States must quickly get started on a space exploration program that will "inspire all of humanity," as the President directed.

To succeed, it will have to be a national mission. It is foolhardy to count on Internet billionaires or enthusiastic college students to carry out a space exploration program for the nation. It is decades past time to return to a credit-based economic policy for investments in long-term projects, most emphatically the space program, which are the legacy, as well as the future, of this nation.

To Fulfill Humanity's Dreams, We Must Get Free of the British Empire!

by William F. Wertz

Mr. Wertz is President of the Schiller Institute USA and an EIR *editorial board member. This edited transcript is adapted from his Nov. 25, 2017 presentation to the LaRouche PAC Manhattan Project Dialogue.*

This week, Helga Zepp-LaRouche said we have made major progress but "we're not in safe waters yet." Today I want to give you a report on the progress the world has made towards a new, just economic order, and at the same time indicate some of the obstacles which still remain and which still must be overcome. On the one hand, progress has been made in the fight against terrorism—despite the inability of the United States and Russia to collaborate directly, due to the British-orchestrated campaign against President Trump for alleged "collusion" with Russia. As well, President Trump has taken initial steps in the direction of collaborating with China's "One Belt, One Road" initiative.

On the other hand, the leadership once provided by Western Christian civilization in the fight for economic justice has in large part been silenced—and even worse, that leadership, in the form of the Roman Catholic Church, has abandoned the perspective of Popes Paul VI and John Paul II, and embraced the genocidal anti-human environmentalism of the British Empire. Moreover, the British Empire, which has been the enemy of the United States of America since its inception, has succeeded since World War II in reducing the United States of America to a virtual satrapy.

If we are to realize the dreams of humanity, it is absolutely necessary to revive the perspective of Popes Paul VI and John Paul II in West European Christian civilization, and thus for the West to engage with China and Russia in a commitment to the common destiny of all humanity, as advocated by Lyndon and Helga LaRouche.

To accomplish this, we must first understand that the British Empire is the enemy of the United States of America, indeed all humanity. To this end, I will show that British geopolitics was responsible for the last two world wars, that the United States of America in the 1930s under President Franklin Roosevelt had plans to fight a two-front war—against Japan *and the British Empire*—and finally, that the British Empire colluded with the architects of its Saudi Arabian satrapy in the September 11, 2001 attack on the United States of America.

This last week, President Assad of Syria visited President Putin in Sochi, Russia. What they have ac-

kremlin.ru

Russian President Vladimir Putin receives Syrian President Bashar al-Assad in Russia.

complished in behalf of humanity is something which we should all applaud, because they have, in a very heroic way, outflanked the British Empire and its policy of regime change, and saved the nation of Syria. But much more than saving the nation of Syria, *per se*, they have saved the principle of national sovereignty, the principle of cooperation among nations for the benefit of all humanity.

Today, very positive developments are taking place in Syria. As you know, two years ago, the Russians intervened in Syria. This was a major flank carried out by President Putin at a point at which forces in the West, including President Obama and Hillary Clinton, through Victoria Nuland, had carried out a Nazi coup in Ukraine. President Putin outflanked that situation and intervened in Syria—before what happened in Libya, and what happened in Iraq, could be replicated in that nation as well.

ISIS and al-Qaeda have been defeated in Syria, and also in Iraq. That does not mean that there is not a continuing threat of terrorism; there is still a need, as President Putin has repeatedly proposed, for a united front internationally against terrorism, just we had a united front against Nazis in World War II. But even without a unified anti-terrorism organization, the fact of the matter is that since President Trump has been in office, and since President Putin has intervened in Syria, a major defeat has been registered against world terrorism and those who have supported that terrorism for their own geopolitical purposes. And that is something which is quite significant, and gives us hope for the future.

Just before this trip of Assad to Sochi, President Trump made an eleven-day trip throughout Asia, going to Japan and South Korea, meeting with President Xi in an historic visit in China, and attending the APEC summit in Vietnam and the ASEAN/East Asia summit in the Philippines. He did not have an official meeting with President Putin. However, after the APEC summit, he lashed out at the fake intelligence officers of former President Obama—Clapper, Comey, and Brennan—for their operation which had been designed on behalf of the British, to prevent President Trump from working with President Putin and with President Xi.

This exposure is something for which we have

Helga Zepp-LaRouche and Lyndon LaRouche.

fought. The LaRouche PAC produced and distributed a dossier entitled "Robert Mueller Is an Amoral Legal Assassin: He Will Do His Job If You Let Him," for the purpose of defeating the attempted *coup d'état* being carried out by British intelligence against the Presidency of the United States, so that President Trump could move forward with an alliance with President Xi, bring the United States into the "One Belt, One Road" initiative, and at the same time, work with President Putin in an international fight against terrorism. These are really one and the same fight.

Lyndon and Helga LaRouche conceived of the World Land-Bridge back in the 1990s, long before China officially adopted this perspective in the fall of 2013. Today, this concept, this grand design, is on the verge of fruition. These two individuals have committed their lives to a love for the truth, a love for humanity, and they have fought over decades, for the benefit of the human race, to create a society which fosters that which distinguishes man from the beast, which is his creativity. And to bring together cultures throughout the world based on the fact that all human beings, as emphasized by Cardinal Nicholas of Cusa, the great theologian and scientist of the 1400s, are "created in the living image of the Creator." That is, man is distinguished from the beasts by his capacity for creativity, and as a result of that, his mission is to be an instrument for the future development of the universe, created by the Creator.

One of the problems we face in the world today is that in Western civilization, the voices who previously spoke in behalf of this perspective, particularly in the

Roman Catholic Church, and the political circles influenced by it, have in large part been silenced, and we have a vacuum. In the past, the policies that are being implemented by President Xi, by Putin, potentially by President Trump, and advocated by Lyndon and Helga LaRouche, were promoted by Pope Paul VI and also by Pope John Paul II.

Two Great Popes

On March 26, 1967, Pope Paul VI issued an encyclical called *On the Development of the Peoples* [*Populorum Progressio*], which we in the LaRouche movement very much endorsed. We held conferences all over the world promoting this idea, because it was completely coherent with the economic development perspective which Lyndon and Helga Zepp-LaRouche have fought for over decades, and which is now coming to fruition with the World Land-Bridge.

What Pope Paul VI said in this encyclical is completely coherent with the viewpoint of President Xi and President Putin, in terms of a "win-win" perspective. He defends national sovereignty, promotes economic development as the new name for peace, and calls for people with different cultures and religions to work together for the common destiny of mankind.

What Paul VI wrote in that encyclical was as follows:

He said that "unchecked liberal capitalism leads to dictatorship rightly … denounced as producing the 'international imperialism of money.'…

"There can be no progress towards the complete development of man without the simultaneous development of all humanity in the spirit of solidarity.…

"The same duty of solidarity that rests on individuals, exists also for nations. … Every nation must produce more and better quality goods to give to all its inhabitants a truly human standard of living and also to contribute to the common development of the

Pope Paul VI

human race."

He then goes on to say that under these conditions, "Developing countries will thus no longer risk being overwhelmed by debts whose repayment swallows up the greater part of their gains. Rates of interest and time for repayment of the loan could be so arranged as not to be too great a burden on either party, taking into account free gifts, interest-free or low-interest loans, and the time needed for liquidating the debts."

He's talking about the creation of a world fund, very similar to the International Development Bank proposed by Lyndon LaRouche in 1975, the New Development Bank created by the BRICS, and other banks which have been created by the Chinese to facilitate the One Belt, One Road policy, which offer long-term credit at low interest rates to facilitate economic development.

Pope Paul VI continues: "The receiving countries could demand that there be no interference in their political life or subversion of their social structures. As sovereign states, they have the right to conduct their own affairs, to decide on their policies, and to move freely towards the kind of society they choose. What must be brought about, therefore, is a system of cooperation freely undertaken, an effective and mutual sharing, carried out with equal dignity on either side, for the construction of a more human world."

Rather than a clash of civilizations, he calls for a dialogue of civilizations, something which we in the Schiller Institute have advocated, for instance. He says, "Between civilizations, as between persons, sincere dialogue indeed creates brotherhood. The work of development will draw nations together in the attainment of goals pursued with a common effort if all … are inspired by brotherly love and moved by the sincere desire to build a civilization founded on world solidarity."

Twenty years later, in 1987, Pope John Paul II wrote

an encyclical called *On Social Concern* [*Sollicitudo Rei Socialis*] on the twentieth anniversary of *Populorum Progressio*, stressing that we must mobilize for the common good of all humanity, and we must create a "civilization of love." He stressed that the quality of creativity is something that has to be promoted, saying: "The right of economic initiative is often suppressed.... The denial of this right, ... absolutely destroys the spirit of initiative, that is to say the creative subjectivity of the citizen.... It often happens that a nation is deprived of its subjectivity, that is to say the 'sovereignty' which is its right...."

Pope John Paul II stresses that at that time there were two "structures of sin." He specifically referred to Marxist collectivism—this is in the period before the collapse of the Soviet Union—and on the other hand, liberal capitalism, which, as we know, was promoted by Adam Smith and the British school of economics:

"Each of the two blocs [the Soviets and the British] harbors in its own way a tendency towards imperialism, ... or towards forms of new-colonialism...." And in contrast to that, he advocates "a firm and persevering determination to commit oneself to the common good.... What is hindering full development is that desire for profit and that thirst for power.... These ... 'structures of sin' are only conquered ... by a diametrically opposed attitude: a commitment to the good of one's neighbor with the readiness ... to 'lose oneself' for the sake of the other instead of exploiting him, and to 'serve him' instead of oppressing him for one's own advantage."

John Paul II concludes that world peace requires "the transformation of mutual distrust into collaboration."

One of the things I stressed at an earlier Manhattan Project meeting, is that China is acting more on Christian principles, even though it's a Confucian society, than Western European civilization is at this moment! I think that you see in these statements, from Pope Paul VI and from Pope John Paul II, a quality of thinking which is not expressed by leaders in Western Europe at this moment, or even in the United States, although President Trump has certainly taken giant steps in that direction.

And that is the reality which we must change. We must create a situation in Western Europe and the United States in which we have leadership of this quality once again, as in the case of Lyn and Helga Zepp-LaRouche. *It is the responsibility of every single citizen.* Lyndon and Helga LaRouche were not born into royalty, they were not born into wealth. They are people who have devoted their entire lives to developing their minds, and have fought with a passion for humanity—and that's what each of us should emulate.

Pope John Paul II

Next, I want to discuss the long wave of British imperialism, which must be ended at this point in human history. Lyndon LaRouche at one point stressed that after the creation of the first nation-states, in France under Louis XI (reigned 1461-1483), and then later under Henry VII (1485-1509) in England, the problem was that the sovereign nation-state system did not become hegemonic throughout the world. Instead, they were forced into a symbiotic relationship with the still-dominant imperial system. Therefore, it was not possible to forge a community of principle among a family of sovereign nation-states throughout the globe. This is the problem identified by both Paul VI and John Paul II. After the "structure of sin" known as the Soviet imperial system collapsed in 1989-1991, there were those, including Francis Fukuyama in his book, *The End of History*, who believed that history was over, because there had been a final victory for liberal capitalism, that we had a unipolar world, and this unipolar world was going to prevail from this point on.

But that has not happened. Instead, what we've seen is that the Chinese and the Russians, in particular, have begun to realize a policy on behalf of all humanity—not a geopolitical policy, not an imperial policy—but a policy that offers hope to humanity in opposition to the British Empire, which has in large part captured the United States of America. The only way we're going to ensure we're in safe waters, is to the extent to which we eliminate the remaining "structure of sin," the British Empire, altogether, and the United States and the rest of Western European civilization is liberated from the British Empire and joins with China, Russia and other countries in creating a new, truly human paradigm. That's the task before us.

Map from Mackinder's The Geographical Pivot of History.

The Disease of Geopolitics

I now want to deepen our understanding of the British imperial system. An imperial system is primarily a financial system which loots human beings and resources through what is called "primitive accumulation" out of a thirst for power on the part of a ruling oligarchy. It's a system of Zeus, who wanted to deny human beings hope in the future, deny scientific development and technology, in order to maintain dominance over all other human beings: That's the system of imperialism. And particularly after World War II, that imperial system has persisted through the financial control of the City of London and of Wall Street, which has functioned as a Trojan horse of the British system in the United States from its inception.

The British have had the intention of taking over the United States since they were thrown out during the American Revolution. As we know, they burned the White House in 1814, during the War of 1812; they supported the Confederacy in order to balkanize the United States and destroy the Union.

But after Lincoln's assassination in 1865, they realized that they had to use other methods to reassert their control, and that entailed defeating the American System of economics of Alexander Hamilton, arguing falsely that the American system of economics is that of Adam Smith. It entailed a direct attack on creativity by people such as Bertrand Russell. It entailed the attack on sovereignty by H.G. Wells in his *Open Conspiracy*. What the British feared most was that the United States would begin to work with other nations throughout the world, and create a combination which would defeat the British Empire as a whole. To prevent that from happening, the British imperialists launched an operation to gain control of, and to destroy the United States of America, and other nations which dared to adopt American System methods as pioneered by Alexander Hamilton, to develop their peoples and to defend their sovereignty. Geopolitics was a means by which British imperial circles attempted to prevent the emergence of a combination of sovereign nations, led by the United States, which would be capable of destroying their power. Halford Mackinder, who is known as the father of British geopolitics, gave a speech to the Royal Geographical Society, published in April 1904, in which he and his interlocutors revealed their cult of geopolitical insanity, from behind whose screen the British Empire has connived to produce the catastrophe which has been the past century of world history. The basic idea of Mackinder's geopolitical cult, is that Russia is the geographical "pivot area" of history in Eurasia. It's surrounded by an inner marginal crescent, and then there's an outer, or insular crescent. Mackinder's obsession was to target Russia by controlling the marginal, inner crescent from the outer, or insular area, the islands lying off the Eurasian continent. This lunacy was used to justify the unleashing of two world wars. It was modified after World War II by Bernard Lewis, into the form of an "arc of crisis" surrounding the Soviet Union. The madness has now been continued after the collapse of the Soviet Union, in order to justify the attempt to maintain a unipolar world.

Mackinder saw the development of transcontinental railroads on the Eurasian continent as an existential threat to continuing imperial control. The formation of an Anglo-Japanese alliance was justified as preventing it. In 1894, the British Empire signed a treaty with Japan, called the Anglo- Japanese Treaty of Commerce and Navigation. Within two weeks of signing that treaty—which was only supposed to go into effect after five years, in 1899—on Aug. 1, 1894, the Japanese launched the Sino-Japanese War of 1894-95. Then, in 1902, the Anglo-Japanese alliance was formed, and on Feb. 8, 1904, the Japanese launched the Russo-Japanese War of 1904-05.

Mackinder delivered his speech in 1904 just as Japan launched war against Russia.

In his speech Mackinder says: "The Russian railways have a clear run of 6,000 miles from Wirballen" which today is Virbalis, Lithuania "in the west to Vladivostok in the east. The Russian army in Manchuria is as significant evidence of mobile land-power as the British army in South Africa was of sea-power. True, the Trans-Siberian railway is still a single and precarious line of communication, but the century will not be old before all Asia is covered with railways."

He continues: "Is not the pivot region of the world's politics that vast area of Euro-Asia which is inaccessible to ships, but in antiquity lay open to the horse-riding nomads, and is to-day about to be covered with a network of railways? The full development of her modern railway mobility is merely a matter of time."

He continues: "The oversetting of the balance of power in favor of the pivot state [i.e., Russia], resulting in its expansion over the marginal lands of Euro-Asia, would permit of the use of vast continental resources for fleet-building, and the empire of the world would then be in sight. This might happen if Germany were to ally herself with Russia." That statement has provided a justification for one of the policy objectives of the British Empire up until the present day, thiat is, to prevent any alliance between Germany and Russia.

He goes on: "May not this in the end prove to be the strategical function of India in the British Imperial system? Is not this the idea underlying Mr. [Leo] Amery's conception that the British military front stretches from the Cape [of Good Hope] through India to Japan?"

Later in the ensuing discussion, one of the participants says: "My own belief is that an island state like our own, can, if it maintains its naval power, hold the balance between the divided forces which work on this continental area, and I believe that has been the historical function of Great Britain, since Great Britain was the United Kingdom. Now we find a smaller island state rising on the opposite side of the Eurasian continent, and I see no reason at all to suppose that that state should not be able to exercise on the eastern fringe of the Asiatic continent, a power as decisive and as influential as that which the British Isles, with a smaller population, has exercised over here."

Mackinder responded to this by saying: "I agree that the function of Britain and Japan is to act on the marginal region, maintaining the balance of power there against the expanse of inner forces. I believe that the future of the world depends on the maintenance of this balance of power."

This discussion seeks to justify an Anglo-Japanese imperial alliance in order to maintain control over the globe. That alliance was a deadly enemy not only of Russia and China, but also of the United States, which suffered the consequences of the British promotion of Japanese imperialists at Pearl Harbor in 1941.

War Plan Red

This British strategy was understood by American patriots, who developed plans to wage a simultaneous war against Great Britain and its allies (War Plan Red) and Japan (War Plan Orange).

The thesis of War Plan Red was that Great Britain would try to invade the United States through Canada. Under the plan, the United States forces, which were "Blue," would capture the port city of Halifax, in Nova

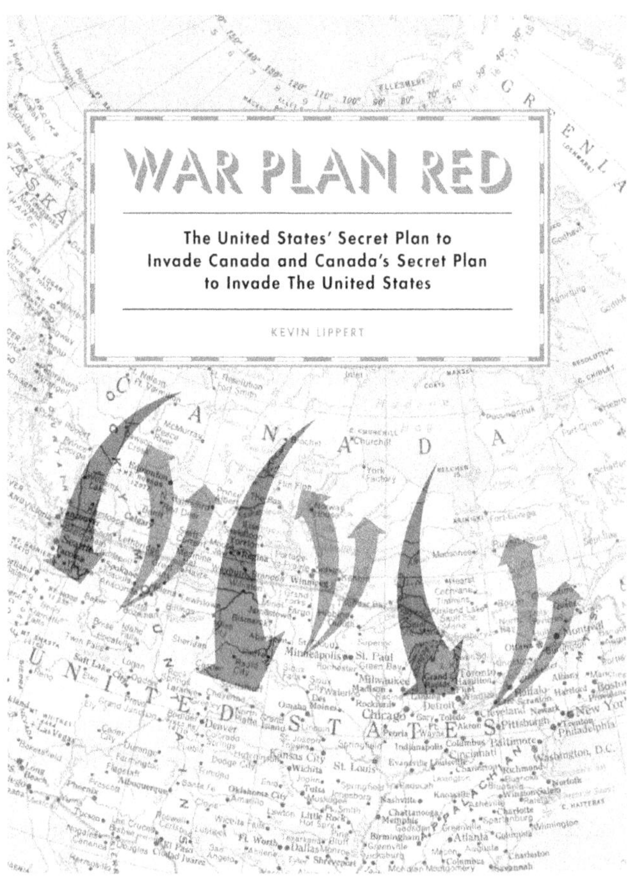

Kevin Lippert's book, War Plan Red.

Scotia, which would cut off the Canadians from their British allies, because Halifax is Canada's main East Coast port. The idea was to seize Canadian power plants near Niagara Falls, followed by a full-scale invasion on three fronts: from Vermont to take Montreal and Quebec; from North Dakota, to take over the railhead in Winnipeg; and from the Midwest to capture the strategic nickel mines in Ontario. And then there would be another operation, by the Navy, to seize the Great Lakes and blockade Canada's Atlantic and Pacific ports. An invasion of Canada's West Coast would go straight up through Bellingham, Washington into Vancouver.

This was not an on-paper war plan. There were actual actions taken in the 1930s when Franklin Roosevelt was President. In 1935, the War Department arranged a Congressional appropriation of $57 million to build three border air-bases disguised as civilian airfields for the purpose of preemptive surprise attacks on Canadian airfields. With these airfields, the United States would be capable of dominating the industrial heart of Canada. This appropriation became public knowledge when it was reported in a front-page article in the *New York Times* on May 1, 1935.

In August 1935, in furtherance of this plan, we also held our largest peacetime military maneuvers *in history*, as 36,000 troops converged at the Canadian border south of Ottawa, with another 15,000 held in reserve in Pennsylvania. The war-game scenario was a motorized invasion of Canada, where defending forces initially repulsed the invading Blue forces, but eventually lost, being outnumbered and outgunned when Blue reinforcements arrived.

This was the *official policy* of the United States through 1939, and the only reason it changed, was because Hitler, who in large part had been supported and brought to power by the British oligarchy in order to attack east against the Soviet Union, unexpectedly attacked west into France, and also attacked Britain. At that point, Prime Minister Churchill realized that he could not defeat the Nazis and preserve the British Empire, unless he could win over the United States to fight with Britain against the Nazis. The perfidious British thus shifted sides at that moment, for pragmatic reasons, to preserve their Empire.

After Roosevelt's untimely death, the very same "Red" countries that War Plan Red was designed to combat, became our intelligence allies in what's now called the Five Eyes—Australia, New Zealand, Canada, Britain, and the United States.

London and 9/11

Let's now turn to the current situation, especially 9/11. After the passage of the Justice Against Sponsors of Terrorism Act, JASTA, and the override of Obama's veto of JASTA, the families of the victims of 9/11 amended their suit to include the Kingdom of Saudi Arabia. From a legal standpoint, the complaint is tailored to take advantage of JASTA to sue the Kingdom of Saudi Arabia directly. And insofar as it does that, the suit is truthful in going after the Saudi role in the 9/11 attacks. What it doesn't do, is to identify the true nature of 9/11, which entailed the British involvement in the 9/11 attack.

The way the suit operates is to say that the various charities and religious organizations which supported al-Qaeda are run by the Kingdom of Saudi Arabia, and therefore the financial and other support by the charities and religious organizations to al-Qaeda was in fact authorized by the Kingdom of Saudi Arabia at the highest level.

I want to focus on one individual featured in the suit, Abdullah Omar Naseef: He was the head of the Muslim World League, and also a member of the Kingdom's Majlis al Shura (government consultative council). He personally met with Osama bin Laden and other founding members of al-Qaeda at the time of al-Qaeda's formation, and agreed that Muslim World League offices would be used as a platform for the new jihad organization, and that attacks would be launched from Muslim World League offices. At the same time, he appointed known founders of al-Qaeda to positions in various organizations in crucial locations where al-Qaeda was to be active. He appointed Wael Hamza Julaidan, a founding member of al-Qaeda, whom the United States designated as a terrorist after 9/11, because he was directing organizations that had provided financial and logistical support to al-Qaeda. In 1989, Wael Hamza Julaidan had been appointed to serve as the head of the Peshawar, Pakistan, office of the Muslim World League.

Naseef also appointed Mohammed Jamal Khalifa, another founding member of al-Qaeda and Osama bin Laden's brother-in-law, to serve as director of the International Islamic Relief Organization (IIRO) in the Far East, which was a major opportunity for al-Qaeda to expand its operations and recruit in that area.

According to the suit: "Shortly after assuming the post, Khalifa used International Islamic Relief Organization funds and resources to support a terrorist cell in the Philippines, which included 9/11 masterminds Khalid Sheikh Mohammad and Ramzi Yousef, in relation to the development of an aviation-based terrorist plot involving the planned simultaneous in-flight deto-

Lawsuit against the Kingdom of Saudi Arabia.

nations of twelve U.S.-flag commercial airline planes. That very plot, often referred to as 'Operation Bojinka,' was adapted by Khalid Sheikh Mohammad, using the knowledge he had acquired during its development about vulnerabilities in the aviation security system, into the September 11th plot."

Now, what is "Operation Bojinka"? This was run in the Philippines, and involved three phases: In Phase I, al-Qaeda operatives intended to assassinate Pope John Paul II at World Youth Day in the Philippines on Jan. 15, 1995. In Phase II, between January 21 and 22, they planned to place bombs on eleven U.S.-bound airplanes. U.S. government investigators estimated that 4,000 people would have been killed had they had gone ahead with this—more than were killed on September 11, 2001. Phase III was to hijack an airplane and crash it into the CIA headquarters in Langley, Virginia.

Investigators also reported that al-Qaeda had an alternative plot, which it felt it was not in a position to carry out at that time, because it would have had to recruit more people, and probably because it would entail greater technical resources than it had at that time. This particular plot, which was discovered during the investigation of Operation Bojinka, was to hijack commercial planes and fly them into the World Trade Center, the Pentagon, the U.S. Capitol, the White House, the Sears Tower in Chicago, and the U.S. Bank Tower in Los Angeles.

The cell that hatched the Bojinka plot included Khalid Sheikh Mohammad (KSM), the reported mastermind of 9/11, and his nephew Ramzi Yousef, who was the mastermind of the 1993 World Trade Center bombing. The plot was funded by the Philippine branch

Abdullah Omar Naseef founded the Oxford Centre for Islamic Studies.

of the IIRO headed by bin Laden's brother-in-law, who was appointed to the position by Dr. Abdullah Omar Naseef, then Secretary General (from 1983-93) of the Muslim World League.

Now let's look at the relationship between our ever-loving British Royal allies, and the key Saudi who facilitated the creation of the cell which plotted 9/11, and who is being sued by American citizens whose family members were killed on 9/11.

In 1985, Abdullah Omar Naseef founded the Oxford Center for Islamic Studies (OCIS) in Great Britain. In 1990, Saudi Prince Bandar bin Sultan Al Saud gave somewhere between $13 and $24 million to the OCIS. In 1993, Britain's Prince Charles became the Patron of OCIS.

As the amended complaint against the Kingdom of Saudi Arabia makes clear, Bandar's wife, Princess Haifa, who is also Prince Turki bin Abdullah Al Saud's sister sent funds beginning in 2000, ultimately totaling $150,000, which were channeled to two of the 9/11 hijackers.

In 2012, Queen Elizabeth II granted the OCIS a Royal Charter. The bin Laden family has endowed the Mohammad bin Laden Chair at the OCIS, named after Osama bin Laden's father.

To this day, the Chair of the Board of Trustees of the Oxford Center for Islamic Studies is none other than its founder, Abdullah Omar Naseef!

The co-chair of the Board of Trustees is Prince Turki, the former director general (1977-2000) of Saudi intelligence, who recruited Osama bin Laden to form al-Qaeda in Afghanistan as part of the British geopolitical "arc of crisis" policy of encircling and dismembering Russia.

As documented in "Robert Mueller Is an Amoral Legal Assassin: He Will Do His Job If You Let Him," it was the British who initiated the persecution of Lyndon LaRouche back in the 1980s; the role of the British in 9/11 has been deliberately covered up; but now British intelligence has been caught red-handed in an attempted *coup d'état* against President Trump. For over two centuries the British Empire has been our enemy. If the world is going to fulfill the dream of mankind, that British Empire *must* be destroyed. Americans must rid themselves of their illusions about the British Empire and our alleged special relationship with Great Britain.

The problem is not Russia; the problem is not China. The problem is the British Empire. Neither China nor Russia is an empire. We only have one "structure of sin" remaining after the collapse of the Soviet Union, and that is British liberal capitalism as we see it on Wall Street and in the City of London today. And if we're going to be able to move forward with a new, just world economic order, it's going to be based upon eliminating the British Empire, getting Americans especially, to understand that the British Empire *is* the enemy and must be destroyed if we are going to have a future in this country, and throughout the world. The New Paradigm which is now emerging requires that the symbiotic relationship between sovereign nation-states and empire is finally broken. This is the decisive point in all human history, and it's crucial that people understand exactly the actual history of the British Empire's ongoing campaign to destroy the United States of America.

V. The Science of Physical Economy

February 8, 2009

THE CONCLUDING DOCUMENT OF A SERIES

Now Comes Economic Time

by Lyndon H. LaRouche, Jr.

*This is the third, and concluding document of an **EIR** series written in this author's supplementary response to a question submitted, with an eye to the subject of a new U.S. economic policy, during the course of an international webcast of January 22, 2009, on the current economic crisis. The titles of the preceding two documents of the series are "Nations as Dynamical" and "The Meaning of Physical Time."*

FOREWORD
What Is Timely Performance?

The following pages are devoted to a summary of the most significant development in the scientific basis for the knowledge and practice of economy since the 1907-1909 period of the closely related work of Albert Einstein and Hermann Minkowski on what was then named "Special Relativity:" the crucial importance of the relativity of time itself. That is the notion of relativity which underlies any actually scientifically competent effort to understand those crucial issues of economic policy which have befuddled the leaders of nations globally since the close of July 2007, the policy-issues which menace the present U.S. Obama government at this present instant.

The validity and importance of those connections for shaping the needed policies for the global economic-breakdown-crisis now in full swing, will become clearer in due course, here.

In fact, the roots of the principle of relativity in modern science, go back to the original discoveries of the principle of gravitation by Johannes Kepler, most notably Kepler's general principle of gravitation, a conception whose discovery is presented, together with the relevant formulation, in painstaking detail, in his ***The Harmonies of the World***. Later, Albert Einstein had credited that discovery by Kepler as the proper foundation for modern physics in general, on the condition that the discovery is situated, as Einstein intended, in the context of the case presented by Bernhard Riemann's 1854 habilitation dissertation, and in the settings of the ancient and modern definitions of the principle of dynamics, as given by the ancient Pythagoreans and modern Gottfried Leibniz.

On the relevance of this matter for U.S. and world economic policy today, I say the following now, and will deal with the matter here again, in appropriate depth, as we approach the concluding pages of this report.

Although there is now widespread, and growing admiration, as also fear, of the perfect success of my July 25, 2007 webcast's forecast of the immediate outbreak of a global economic breakdown-crisis of the present world monetary-financial system, there is little confidence, even in leading U.S. Government circles, for actually adopting and implementing those urgently needed, immediate actions without which the world as we have known it, including our own U.S. political-financial system, would now, assuredly, simply cease soon to exist.

In these pages, I explain that crisis, its causes, and its remedy. When the horrid consequences of failure to heed my warning here, are considered, my forecast may be seen by some thoughtful readers, as, in both theory and practice, the most important piece of writing on economic policy as such which has been written in world history so far. As you shall see here, that is no exaggeration, even in the slightest degree.

I explain.

The customary European civilization's traditional view of history, as it exists in the teachings of schools, universities, and so forth, today, has been chiefly shaped, and also significantly crippled, by resort to the vantage-point of the largely doubtful assumptions of what is widely viewed, retrospectively, as what the Sophists of ancient Greece experienced in their own tragic role as a forerunner of the tragic situation inherent in today's widespread, reductionist opinion. This reductionist legacy has been widely reconciled, still today, with the Sophist-like traditions of Aristotle, as that tradition is typically reflected in the fraudulent, *a-priori* presumptions of Euclidean *a-priori* definitions, axioms, and postulates. Under that pro-Aristotelean scheme, all accounts of history and its consequences, have been degraded to the assumption, that the universe as a whole is to be defined, in both the very large and the very small, by those unfounded assumptions respecting space and time which are consistent with the *a-priori* assumptions of Aristotelean and Euclidean dogma.

That is the same as to say, that the very boundary conditions most often applied to describe every aspect of human life's experience, have been thus premised upon still-prevalent presumptions which have never been proven in fact, and which are, in fact, as I shall indicate in the following chapters of this report, largely absurd from the standpoint of more carefully considered, experimentally validated standards of physical-scientific practice.

Science itself must now come to lead the rescue of

The crucial importance of the relativity of time itself, as discovered by Einstein and Minkowski, are those which have befuddled the leaders of nations globally, since July 2007: These are the policy issues which menace the Obama Administration today. Shown: President Obama with his economic team.

mankind from today's popular expressions of mankind's ancient follies.

On this account, every competent view of the decline of the culture of physical science over the course of more than four recent decades, is faced with accumulated evidence which tends to prove that the ideas common to such as Aristotle, Euclid, and Descartes are not, in fact, merely false, but are ruinously absurd. Yet, for the most part, even our leading universities' tradition of today, continues, still, to defy reason in these matters. They define it *a-priori, axiomatically,* as if by obedience to a babbling Emperor Nero's imperial decree.

For this reason, it is urgent that the 1854 habilitation dissertation of Bernhard Riemann be remembered, especially on account of both that dissertation's opening two paragraphs, and its closing sentence, as having given an urgently needed, new birth to modern science, then, and as being typical of those foundations of what had become the greatest achievements of recent past times. Riemann's dissertation is proven to be indispensable in laying the basis for my own unique achievements, my repeated successes as a long-range economic forecaster.

As the late Albert Einstein had warned, during the last years of his life, the net effect of the revolution in science launched by Riemann, was a revolutionary

As Bernhard Riemann (left) warned, science is never science when it is merely formal; the subject of science is man, as Riemann and his followers, Albert Einstein (center) and Max Planck, understood.

change in the notions of space and time. Unfortunately, even the Hermann Minkowski who had certainly earned much credit for his 1907-1909 role, as an ally of Albert Einstein, in promoting the concept of what was then known as "special relativity," made the significant error of substituting the proposal for a Lobatchevskyian geometry for a truly anti-Euclidean, Riemann standpoint; but, nonetheless, science, still today, should not forget Minkowski's resonant utterance in his famous lecture on relativity, that Einstein's presentation of a case of "special relativity" showed that "space by itself and time by itself" no longer existed for the future of physical science.[1]

In the following pages, you will encounter evidence of another great quality of Riemann's work for contemporary science, its essential moral significance for dealing with the presently onrushing threat of a very early general physical-economic breakdown-crisis of this planet as a whole.

Riemann, Planck, and Einstein

It happens, by no accident, that the matter of the relativity of time could not be approached successfully, except in a very special way. As I shall indicate the reasons for that here, the relativity of time could not be shown without situating the real issues involved from the standpoint of reference of what I have defined as a science of physical economy, the subject of my own notable professional expertise. Hence, that aspect of relativity is of crucial importance for identifying the causes and remedies for the presently onrushing, global economic breakdown-crisis.

On this account, it must be said here, that a science is never science when it is merely formal, as Riemann warned in the case of formal mathematics.[2] Therefore, to advance knowledge in a new, crucial topical area, it

---

1. Speaking of a highly relevant matter here, in formal terms, the introduction of a non-Euclidean geometry was actually conceived by Carl F. Gauss during his student days of association with his mentors Abraham Kästner and A.W. von Zimmermann. Kästner, the initiator of a modern, explicitly anti-Euclidean geometry, was the pioneer in rejecting any likeness of a Euclidean geometry. On the later issue of the claims of Janos Bolyai, see two of Gauss's letters to Farkas Bolyai (Gauss's old friend and Janos' father), in Carl F. Gauss *Der "Fürst der Mathematiker" in Briefen und Gesprächen* (Munich: Verlag C.H. Beck, 1990), pp.137n, 139-140. Unfortunately, the third of the leading, pre-Riemann advocates of a non-Euclidean geometry (Kästner, Gauss, Janos Bolyai, and N. Lobatchevsky), Janos was not consoled by Gauss's generous words on the subject of the conflict. Gauss's own reply to Farkas Bolyai on this matter, reflects an important weakness in Gauss's approach to presenting his own accomplishments (under the politically unfavorable circumstances established by Napoleon Bonaparte's reign, and, later, until the death of the hoaxster Augustin Cauchy, that at a time which, unfortunately, coincided with the onset of Gauss's own terminal years).

To read Gauss's private intentions in such matters, it is essential to recognize something important of Gauss as coming to the surface in the work of Bernhard Riemann and Alexander von Humboldt's protégé Lejeune Dirichlet.

2. Cf. the opening two paragraphs and concluding sentence of Riemann's famous 1854 habilitation dissertation.

is indispensable, first, to locate that physical subject-matter which is most relevant, functionally, to the principles being considered, human economic behavior.

The subject here, is, therefore, man, and, especially, the follies of currently widespread popular and related opinion.

In the matter at hand, there can be no competent treatment of the subject of economy which does not, by its nature, provide a truly integral picture of the functional interplay of physical principle and the underlying principles of action of the human will. This can be achieved only in the subject of a science of physical economy, my own exceptional specialty.

Therefore, I have proceeded as I have done in what this present article completes as a series of three small-booklet-sized EIR features, a series prompted by the occasion of an important, highly relevant question posed to me publicly during my January 22nd international webcast.

I. How to Make a Forecast

Mankind changes the physical value, and therefore the proper *physical measure* of physical space-time, through the combination of physical-scientific and associated progress in the rate at which mankind changes the tempo of all other physical processes on this planet, and, now, recently, beyond that. This matter of principle is most clearly shown in the effects of discovery and implementation respecting the physical increase, or decadence, of the human species' special kind of power in the universe, per capita and per square kilometer of relevant territory.

Notably, the scientific description of the pathetic incompetence of all current opponents of science-driven increase of the human population, is shown in that they implicitly deny the fact, that failure to progress scientifically in growth of the economy, as our U.S.A. has failed, consistently, during the recent forty years (1968-2008),[3] means that the fate of mankind has been in the hands of influences akin to those kinds of accelerating processes of collapse, through attrition, which are, categorically, an imitation of the familiar boundary presented to us in the case of lower forms of life: as boundaries in the sense of potential for the relative, ecological population-densities which are encountered among the sub-human forms of life. In fact, this has also been the case with all known oligarchical cultures of European and related experience since the destruction, through effects of salination, of the Mesopotamian, bow-tenure culture of ancient Sumer, or, the doom of that Biblical Sodom and Gomorrah which appears to have enjoyed a certain salty kind of revival in current modern times.[4]

Mankind as a species, is, indeed, *potentially* subject to those "forces" of ecological attrition in population-densities, the which are familiar to us among the populations of the lower forms of life. For example: we, admittedly, sometimes encounter a transitional condition, between animal ecology and so-called human "ecology," in the domain of animal husbandry, and also among populations of plants and their infectious diseases. *However*, these later, seemingly exceptional categories of experience with animal husbandry, and the like, are effects of human culture, rather than being endemic to the animal species considered in this matter.

Thus, without the impact of those aspects of scien-

---

3. Since the combination of the 1967-68, successive collapse of the British pound sterling, U.S. President Johnson's capitulation of March 1, 1968, and the riotous outburst of the Spring, Summer, and Autumn of that year. U.S. fiscal year 1967-1968 was the beginning of a net collapse in the basic economic infrastructure of the U.S. economy: we have been going downhill in physical economy ever since. The 1968 election of President Richard Nixon has been the beginning of the end reached in today's aftermath of eight years of the worst U.S. Presidency in U.S. history since the end of that British puppet known as the Confederacy. Even Presidencies such as that of relics of the Confederacy, Theodore Roosevelt and Woodrow Wilson, were not as thoroughly rotten as that under George Shultz's puppet George W. Bush, Jr.

4. If we, for convenience, compare the "cultures" of mankind with those attributed to the higher apes, we must recognize that the human species is a relatively poor performer as a species, until we take efficiently into account the effect of the human creative-mental powers which are peculiar to all mankind, but absent in all lower forms of life, including the apes. These are powers not to be confused with the mere problem-solving capabilities of dogs and apes, for example. Creativity is not a matter of "knacks," but of discovery and employment of new *universal physical principles*. All forms of life are inherently clever, relative to today's right-wing free-market ideologues, such as Hank Paulson, but none, excepting mankind, is actually, potentially, efficiently creative. Which is why we must say, of all of the co-thinkers of Paulson and cultish groups, such as the dupes of the American Enterprise Institute (AEI), who have failed the United States and its citizens so miserably, over recent decades: they might have been better employed in attempts to learn to behave as if they were actually devoted to human interests. AEI today typifies the rebirth, after Pearl Harbor day, of those anti-Franklin Roosevelt associations which changed their outer clothing, but have otherwise remained, inwardly, today, the same traditionally, pro-Mussolini and pro-Hitler, as they were, overtly, up to the events at Pearl Harbor. The Franklin Roosevelt haters of today, such as Felix Rohatyn and Britain's drug-trafficking George Soros, typify that legacy.

tific and technological progress which increase the potential relative population-densities of societies, the human populations must tend to suffer a decline which verges upon catastrophic demographic and related effects, as we have suffered so, most conspicuously, under the regime of George W. Bush, Jr. In other words, the practical issue presented to statecraft, is a matter of the balance between the decline of the human condition, due to attrition, and, otherwise, as resisted, or even overcome, by the increase of human potential relative population-density through the realized benefits of periods of the acceleration of investment in the fruits of scientific and related progress.

If that is considered, we should seek to craft a set of scales comparable to my economic "Triple Curve," (*Figure 1*) which corresponds, as a representation, to this array of conflicting effects within the bounds of human experience as such. We can already, thus, present a notion of relative time, distinct from clock-time, in terms of the net effects of the time-measured rate of change in the potential relative population-density of both the U.S. and world populations. The prospect of the effect which we will have represented, approximately, by such statistical schemes, presents us with a useful indication of the existence of a more ominous process in development, (the effect of realized investment, or relative lack of investment), in relatively capital-intensive scientific progress.

The effect of wisdom on this account, would be to measure the rate of the physical-economic effect of the passage of clock-time in social (e.g., "demographic") terms.

Perhaps the most startling, and relevant empirical effects with which the novice is confronted in studying that approach, is the effect of the promotion, or lack of promotion, of increase of what is termed "energy flux-density" of the applied sources of power employed to maintain and improve the rate of productivity in the population generally. Suddenly, thus, the practically expressed powers of the typical human mind, when expressed by the society as a unit, become a measure of the functional relationship between the trend toward rise, or fall, of the *relative potential relative population-density* of the society, and the variations in the rate of time during which any among the physical effects of this process unfold.

In other words: "In what condition will the society be, in these terms of reference, at a certain future date?" "At what rate will that change occur?" Instead of asking

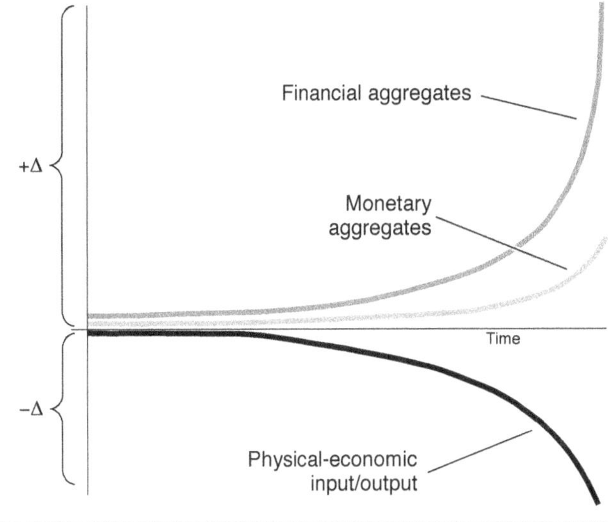

FIGURE 1

LaRouche's Triple Curve

to see the U.S.A. in the year A.D. 2025, ask, in what year will the U.S.A. actually reach a condition which could be reached potentially in the year 2025, or, perhaps, only 2050? Where does the zero-point of hovering lie, between net growth and the net collapse, which has been the characteristic trend in the economies of the U.S.A. and Europe since the tumultuous developments of 1968?

My Own Forecasting

All my forecasts, since my short-term, mid-1956 forecast of a deep early 1957 recession, have been of that type. These are typical of the method of forecasting, premised on Riemannian conceptions, which I have employed with such relative success, relative, that is, to the relatively failed methods of forecasting adopted by other ostensibly known economists ploughing the field during approximately a half-century to date.

This was the basis for my warning in Summer 1956, which was based upon my systemic evidence of a then onrushing relatively awesome U.S. economic recession, a recession centered in the evidence I considered in respect to the exemplary case of the foolish practices of the auto industry's Robert McNamara, et al., at that time. The evidence of the contrast between the physical trends built into systemic practice during the mid-1950s, sufficed to show me clearly that a deep recession was due to hit with exceptional force approximately February 1957. It happened then exactly as I had warned. This success became the model of reference

EIRNS/Stuart Lewis

All of LaRouche's economic forecasts, from the 1957 recession, through his July 25, 2007 forecast of the current global breakdown crisis, are premised on Riemannian conceptions. LaRouche is shown here, during his July 25, 2007 webcast.

for the form of construction of my first long-range forecast, made in 1959-60, of a probable deepening U.S. recession during the late 1960s, *unless*, first, the current (pre-President John F. Kennedy) trend in policies were reversed by the middle of the 1960s, and, unless, second, a few years later, that the wrong post-Kennedy policy-drift were reversed by about the beginning of the 1970s.

In effect, the assassination of President Kennedy, coupled with what had been the ouster of Britain's Macmillan, also with the British and German Liberals' pushing out of Germany's Chancellor Konrad Adenauer, and also the repeated, earlier, and later, attempts at assassination of President Charles de Gaulle, typify the way in which Anglo-American, and related continental European policy-making practices were changed, for the worse, from that time onward. The changes shaped by 1962-1964 developments of this pattern, led to the 1968-1971 economic crisis which I had then foreseen as an approximately, early-1970s effect. The effect which actually came as the result, was the 1971-1981 collapse of the U.S. dollar and what proved to be the worse, correlated outcome: that poisonous cultural phenomenon of the so-called "68ers," with their neo-malthusian hatred of progress, which all amounted, in effect, to a catastrophe-in-the-making, from which the world gripped, at large, by monetary inflation, has never actually recovered, up to the present date.

These forecasts of mine were the result of exercises made explicitly according to the principle of dynamics, that of both Gottfried Leibniz, and that of the Bernhard Riemann on whose work all of my forecasts to date have been premised as in respect to scientific method. This has been a method of forecasting which not only echoes Leibniz's and Riemann's method of dynamics, but, also, the argument which Percy Shelley presented in the concluding paragraph of his *A Defence of Poetry*. That concluding paragraph from Shelley's work, may be considered as the true, deepest "secret" of both competent economic forecasting and related statecraft, a secret which has remained unknown to virtually all of the leading governments and universities of the world today. This argument is also the "secret" on which the immediate survival of global civilization depends today.

What I have written here so far, already goes a considerable distance toward suggesting the direction of my thinking. The point is, that that method, which I have employed, over decades, for forecasting, exposes the way in which governments and other relevant parties have come to their present, ruinous habits of thinking, as academics, or, otherwise, the bad habits, fit for deposit in a bad bank, which are the essential, proximate cause of the great crisis which menaces all civilization, immediately, today.

Those Were the Preliminaries

It was the adoption, as by Wall Street influentials, of the self-destructive, Liberal ideology traced in origins to the Liberalism of Paolo Sarpi and Adam Smith, which, by replacing the protectionist principles of the U.S. Federal Constitution, has caused the recent decades' dive of the U.S.A., and most other nations of the world, toward a "new dark age." The recent decades' result, has been the harvest of the rotten fruit of that season of that more recent, new wave in the Anglo-Dutch Liberalism which has abounded increasingly in Trans-Atlantic and some other cultures, since the middle of the 1960s. This Liberal ideology which has ruined us, has been most often expressed in a relatively more conspicuous way, by the tendency of people, and their nations, to react to the passage of time by stubborn efforts to impose a willful, foolish kind of practice, even mere fads, rather than seeking out the necessary changes in their mental habits, as individuals, or groups of persons, changed habits which would be an appropriate response to the existing and oncoming situations.

Those fools said, in effect: "This is my culture!" "This is our tradition!" Fools said, in effect: "This is the way we have dumped the traditions, such as those of Benjamin Franklin and Alexander Hamilton, which we had adhered to in the past." Our fools said: "This is my circle's opportunity to impose our way of thinking at the expense of those who tend to think and act differently!" "You will see! We are going to come out on top, whatever it takes!" Such is the pathetic whimpering we hear from leading circles inside the U.S.A., in the capitals of western and central Europe, in a confused government of a Russia guided by London-steered, "sub-prime" Minister Kudrin, and elsewhere, today.[5]

To describe such people, or groups, as being reasonable, would be to insult their native intelligence. Their inclinations have had more of the character of the stub-

We are not threatened by "global warming," writes LaRouche, "unless solar receptors and windmills could bring that result about; we are, in fact, on the verge of the cyclical advent of a threatened new increase of that continuing ice age which has been in process for an estimated 2 million years."

born ways of a self-doomed species, like as the salty Biblical folk of Sodom and Gomorrah, than actual human beings.

Today, the follies of Sodom and Gomorrah are echoed by what is called "environmentalism." Indeed, there is no better way to ensure the overheating of the environment than to turn the planet into a deadly wasteland by covering vast acreages with silly windmills and worse solar receptors.

Here, in reality, we are not actually threatened by "global warming," unless solar receptors and windmills could bring that result about; we are, in fact, on the verge of the cyclical advent of a threatened new increase of that continuing ice age which has been in a process, typical of such developments, of flowing and ebbing, back and forth, on this planet, that for what may be estimated, for purposes of our discussion, as an estimated two millions years, whereas what have been recently the leading currents of economic policy-shaping, are committed to so-called "free energy" policies which would, if continued, transform the planet into a desert, and bring on the intended (as by London's Duke of Edinburgh) collapse of the world to a world degraded to such a state of brutish human populations, all that according to that "salty, bad Lot" Duke's avowed intention to reduce the world's population rapidly from over

____

5. Despite the immediate confirmation of the warning delivered in my July 25, 2007 forecast of an onrushing, global general breakdown crisis of the existing world economy, and despite the skyrocketting, and most dramatic evidence in support of that forecast throughout the entire span of developments through the present date, Russia's government refused to acknowledge this reality through December 2008, while "sub-prime" Minister Kudrin has just announced a perspective which is frankly insane in its presumptions and conclusions, and potentially suicidal for Russia as a nation. This development has been under careful, global study, as a matter of strategic counterintelligence, in U.S. interests, against the British empire, for some time. I do not speak idly in these matters.

6.5 billions to less than 2 billions persons. Sodom and Gomorrah all over again, but, this time, on a vastly wider, and much more sinful scale.

The evidence is clearly available; but, many people deny these facts, nonetheless, because they have been brainwashed into the inherently tragic, neo-malthusian mythologies of the Olympian Zeus of Aeschylus's ***Prometheus Bound***. The older generation of malthusians, those from the ranks of the "68ers," required the lies they told themselves, and also others, to induce them to adopt neo-malthusian mass-murderous policies for the planet at large. A portion of these present-day pro-malthusian generations, younger than those "68ers," has no evidence, but only their own, fanatically insane wish to believe. The latter are, in effect, clearly insane, victims of the epidemic mass-insanity which, taken together with George Soros's legalized drug-trafficking, is presently, the greatest of all particular forms of endemic threats to mankind throughout this planet.

Similarly, during the middle to latter part of Europe's Fourteenth Century, financial practices like those adopted by contemporary London and Wall Street, plunged a Europe dominated by the Venetian usury of that century's Lombard League, and all of Europe, into the worst "new dark age" of the medieval period, a world-wide "dark age" of the type presently onrushing to the brink of a general, chain-reaction, planetary collapse, today.

The point which I am emphasizing, and must emphasize, here, is to be recognized as a certain principle of physical science.

II. Mankind's New Age of Reason

Looking backwards in time, for a view of the way in which the recent advance of science and related practice (including visits of our captive scientific apparatus to Mars) has brought us to the verge of beginning to manage the Solar System today, the most relevant fact in the history of science, is the degree to which—*when science prevails over un-science*—mankind's power in and over the universe is increasing, as a trend. This progress should be viewed as translated not merely into the form of mankind's increased power, but, more emphatically, mankind's responsibilities.

This point which I have just made here, is an updated definition of the practical meaning of the term: *"a physical science of human ecology."*

More than ever before that time, the outcome of progress in this direction had been indicated by, most notably, earlier, Nicholas of Cusa, Johannes Kepler, Pierre de Fermat, Gottfried Leibniz, and, later, Bernhard Riemann, and, later, by the leading scientists of that subsequent age of Planck, Vernadsky, and Einstein, which was introduced by Riemann's 1854 habilitation dissertation. This legacy of science, has given us a recent, and continuing new meaning to the competent use of the term *science* itself.

We have thus, with the impact typified by Riemann's habilitation dissertation, entered into a new phase of what must be termed "universal history," that in the sense of the most profound implications of that name. In this fresh view of modern universal history, we have moved from belief in the Solar system as acting on man, to Promethean man's acting according to the principle of ***Genesis*** 1, to change the universe as we know it, and as we must guide our practice of mankind in that direction.

In my method of forecasting, I emphasize the relevance of the existence of a certain kind of moving point on the relevant statistical scale. That point has the character of a physical function, rather than representing the fruit of a simple statistic. The "point" has two aspects. First there is the concept of a net increase of a society's potential relative population-density, as measurable per capita and per square kilometer of relevant territory. So, secondly, we are interested in knowing that which determines the rate of increase of that potential relative population-density. We are properly concerned with the net rate of increase of that potential over time.

That presents the idea of the implied measurement in a general preliminary way. Better were to start from Vernadsky's notions of the respective pre-biotic domain, the Biosphere's domain, and, then, the Noösphere's domain. We are, then, concerned with the rate of increase of the human potential relative population-density as measured against that value's implied, prerequisite, abiotic domain, and Biosphere pre-conditions for that current rate of increase of estimated potential relative population-density.

The rate of estimated current rate of net increase of potential relative population-density for a society as a whole, then defines an implied standard for the measurement of physical, as distinct from "clock" time.

The notion of that preliminary approach to estimating the function for increase of potential relative population-density, then implies a rate of interaction between human existence and changes in the portion of universe within which the increases in rate of net increase of potential relative population-density are situated.

As we attempt to refine this calculation, the complications with which we are confronted, increase: first, within the immediate bounds of Earth and its local Solar-system environment, then Kepler's Solar system, and so on, outward and deeper. Then, we encounter theology, but in a certain fashion. Turn to the pages of **Genesis** 1, and look at that chapter's content in the fashion of a Moses who was able to walk in, and then out of the Pharaoh's palace with, considering his messages of a new round of pestilences delivered, an apparent impunity which Moses enjoyed, in coming and going on those occasions, and in that implicitly perilous fashion. Then read **Genesis** 1 again, but not as the devotees of Aristotle might have done later, or the Elmer-Gantry-like "fundamentalists" of today.

Contrary to the putative Aristotle known to Philo of Alexandria, the Creator actually did generate the universe (after all, it does really exist in the quality of something which has been, and is being created!), and according to Moses, man and woman are "made in the likeness" of that Creator. Moreover, if it is the real universe that we are discussing in that way, the real universe as we know it, is *in a process of continuing creation*. That means generating higher states of existence than could be adduced from an existing state of existence. That means, contrary to the hoaxsters Clausius, Grassmann, Kelvin, et al., the universe's form of continued existence is *anti-entropic*, not some silly system under the imagined rule of universal entropy.

We also observe that man and woman, unlike all lower forms of life, are, in fact, *creative* in that ontological sense of anti-entropy. Since Moses is referring to man and woman, he intends to convey the idea that the Creator represents, or should represent, continuing creation in the image of his servants, man and woman. Philo of Alexandria, the friend of the Christian Apostle Peter, said as much against the Aristoteleans of the known historical time of Jesus and his Apostles. As a great, recently deceased rabbi insisted to me: *The Messiah will not arrive according to the likeness of a train-schedule, but when the Creator decides.* The implication is the worshiper's reaction to this advice: "Please come, as soon as possible!"

(It is necessary to approach subject-matters of that type with a special quality of humble tone of affection.)

Put the line of discussion I have been employing in this chapter thus far, as follows. For the next minutes, I will postpone the subject of physical-economy as such, in order to prepare some essential elements of physical-science background, within which terms I shall then situate the subject of physical economy as such, and, after I have presented that crucial scientific material, we shall then turn to the matter of the role of monetary values within the setting of the principles of physical economy.

The Relevant Case of Helen Keller

So, that much said as preliminary, turn to the core of the science of the matter.

As I have been reminded by an associate who reminded me of Louis Pasteur's point about scientific method, the true evidence of the experienced existence of physical time, as distinct from clock time, is to be located in a category of phenomena which prove the existence of something not only exceptional, but ostensibly contrary to all that has seemed usual.

So, in the case of the discovery of the notion of physical time, reference to the exceptional implications of the famous case of Helen Keller, implicitly forces the thoughtful discoverer to see the way to bridge the gap between time, as located in *a-priori* notions of sense-certainty, and the reality which is that physical reality, rather than clock-time, which exists in the unseen domain of a physical actuality.

This comparison is suggested by looking back to crucial features of Kepler's original discovery of the general principle of Solar-system gravitation, which occurred, as Kepler accounts for this, through the sense of the ontological irony of seeing and hearing (harmonically) the organization of the Solar system. Once we recognize that Kepler's uniquely original discovery of a principle of gravitation, expresses a method of thinking which carries over into all profound physical discoveries in general, we will have taken the first step toward access to a sense of physical-scientific certainty in the matter of physical time.

First of all, such intellectual experiences as those, of the principle of irony specific to the experience of principles underlying the phenomena of space-time. Or, as the same thought appears as the concluding sentence of Bernhard Riemann's 1854 habilitation dissertation: *we depart the department of mathematics for physics.*

Once we accept what should be the obvious fact about the all-too-obvious, our sense-experiences, as

"How did Helen Keller conduct dialogues involving ideas, in her special way, with persons she could neither see, nor hear? Kepler's uniquely original discovery of gravitation, provides an implied illustration of the same method expressed by that Helen Keller."

such, that sense-perception as such is merely the instrumentation of the real universe we are experiencing, we have touched that threshold of valid science known, explicitly, to the greatest among our modern scientists, such as Kepler, Leibniz, Riemann, and Albert Einstein. As in all competent experimentation, actual knowledge is the product of the mind's power to synthesize that efficient, but unsensed reality, the which we must adduce from the mere phenomena. Thus, honestly competent sense requires the construction of a kind of intellectual "bridge" to what must become known, but is not sensed: one might suggest the example of the catenary, the funicular bridge which was essential for Brunelleschi's successful construction of the cupola of Florence's **Santa Maria del Fiore**. My own personal discovery, while an adolescent, of the anti-Euclidean principle of physical geometry, is an example of the same principle of all actually scientific knowledge. *Knowledge of a principle is never an intellectual fantasy; it is an idea*

whose action enables one to produce a unique kind of actual (e.g., "crucial experimental") effect, but one which had been previously unknown within the scope of previously known principles. In that sense, all physical science is experimental, that in the sense of what Riemann identifies as the quality of *unique experiments* specific to discoveries of physical principle.

Such was the quality of the relevant achievement in Albert Einstein's recognition of the unique validity of the original discovery of the principle of gravitation, by Kepler. That said, we have thus placed ourselves in the proximity of an added discovery, the discovery of the concept of *physical time*.

So, as I have pointed out on numerous occasions, we have the case of Kepler's uniquely original discovery of *the physical principle of* gravitation, which is reported by him in his **The Harmonies of the World**. That, Kepler's method, for example, is the way we may actually know a true physical principle, as distinct from the pathetically contemplative act of merely choosing to believe in "a merely mathematical explanation." The present need to define the concept of physical time, presents us with a challenge of that same type.

For example, how did Helen Keller conduct dialogues involving ideas, in her special way, with persons she could neither see, nor hear? Kepler's uniquely original discovery of gravitation, provides an implied illustration of the same method expressed by that Helen Keller. Now consider Kepler's discovery in such terms of reference. Then, consider, in that light, how the method expressed by the method of discovery by Kepler is to be applied to the matter of the notion of physical time.

There is another, kindred sort of consideration to be emphasized afresh at this immediate juncture.

All valid discoveries of universal scientific principles, occur as discovery of something which exists efficiently, but as if outside, and above previously established conceptions. The ideas of physical space, as distinct from open space, or physical time from clock time, are examples of this. Hence, the dynamics of physical-space, rather than space, and of space-time rather than clock time. So, in the case of Kepler's discovery of gravitation, we have physical space, rather than Euclidean or Cartesian space. So, we have the case of physical-time, rather than clock time. These are not matters of verbal hyphenation; consider what it is which they reflect, in each such, or comparable species of instance.

Think of what I have referenced above, as the case of Louis Pasteur. In Kepler's discovery of gravitation, it is the juxtaposition of what are, conceptually, the relative incommensurables of the notions of sight, and of the harmonics of hearing, which are combined by Kepler's mind to form, as if by some higher quality of irony, the mentally visible, a physically efficient shadow of a universal physical principle of gravitation.

That said, return attention to Helen Keller's insight into the thinking of another person. When we are enabled to recognize the common implication shared among the variety of cases which I have just identified above, that when they are considered as a subject-matter of some general principle, we have the first general approximation of the kind of thinking needed to grasp, accurately, the concept of space-time. We now proceed from that point as follows.

I shall now deal with that notion in those limited terms. Subsequently, I shall address the deeper implications at a later point in this present report.

Anti-Entropy: Dynamics in Space-Time

The discovery of experimentally validatable principles of nature, begs for the notion of some demonstrable ordering-principle in the configuration among those principles. The appropriate reply to that implied question always comes back, sooner or later, to the fact that what we are enabled to recognize as the ordering among the principles of such a sought-for configuration, lies within the human mind. It is not necessarily a copy of the biology of the human brain, but, assuredly, a reflection of the process expressed as man's increased power to exist in the universe.

In general, in this location, it is permitted, and most convenient to take a few short-cuts in illustrating the point immediately at hand.

One of the most convenient of those short-cuts, is to be found in considering the evidence bearing on the relative "negative entropy" of effect, as man's use of heat-sources moves upward from incident sunlight at the surface of the Earth, through burning of simple fuels, into coal, coke, petroleum and natural gas, into nuclear fission and thermonuclear fusion. It is not the number of calories that defines the relative power to do work,

but, rather, the density of that power to do work, expressed in units of heat-equivalent, that measured per square centimeter of cross-section of the flow of the heat-process being considered. Compare this with the cases of the species-fertility of not only the orders and species of animal life, but of varying combinations of species sharing in the dynamics (that in the sense of Leibniz and Riemann) of a particular sort of habitat.

However, such illustrations put aside, our crucial concern at this point in the report, is, as Leibniz exposed the fraud of Descartes on the subject of physical space-time, is, as Leibniz showed the need to focus attention on the order of increase of the power of the effect which is expressed by any specific dynamic system of mankind to exist.[6]

There are two considerations posed here. One, is the order of matters in the universe, relative to mankind, on the presumption that this order pre-exists. The other, is posed in the form of a question: to what degree does discovery go further than discovering the usefulness of pre-existing principles in the universe, or his local portion of it; is mankind actually generating newly added universal physical and related principles in this universe? To what degree is a discovery merely a discovery, and to what degree is the very existence of a discovered phenomenon a product of the creative powers of mankind? In other words, does the practical existence of the discovered principle exist with the adoption of that principle of action by mankind? The result of the progress of mankind in exploring the domains of nuclear fission and thermonuclear fusion, poses exactly such general types of new forms of questions for modern science, still today.

The desire for some form of ordering-principle amid the evidence to be considered along those lines, a desire which such thoughts engender, is a mark of the passion which motivates true discoveries of those principles which are not sensory objects themselves, but which produce the form of movement of sensory objects.

Such is the form of the argument which leads toward comprehension of the notion of physical space-time. For a very significant reason, this conception can be reached only from the vantage-point of understanding ourselves as being uniquely creative individuals, that in the sense of Riemann's admonition to leave the depart-

---

6. Leibniz, "Critical Thoughts on the General Part of the Principles of Descartes," (1692) and in "Specimen Dynamicum" (1995) Loemker, ed. (Dodrecht/Boston/London: Kluwer Academic Publishers, 1989).

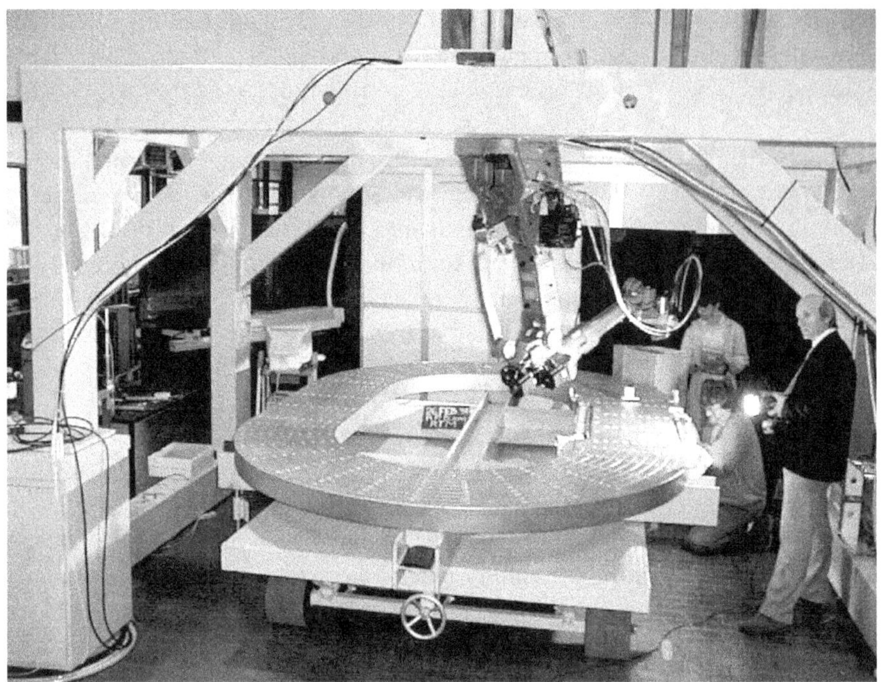

The progress of mankind in exploring the domains of nuclear fission and thermonuclear fusion, raises such questions as, "To what degree is a discovery merely a discovery, and to what degree is the existence of a discovered phenomenon a product of the creative powers of mankind?" Shown, ITER'S laser welding of conductor cover plates, for the Toroidal Field Model Coil Project.

the notions of animal ecology. This distinction is expressible in terms of a contrast between what would be named, in relatively popular terms, as *a relatively fixed ecological potential* (i.e., *entropic*) for that population, as opposed to the inherently anti-entropic characteristic of any naturally healthy culture of the human species.

So, since the still continuing 1967-68 downshift in the ratio of new infrastructure to the depletion of formerly established infrastructure, there has been a relative long-term decline in the physical economy in the U.S. economy. There was the downshift of this sort which dominated the 1968-1974 interval in the U.S. economy, followed by a greatly accelerated margin of decay and decline under the 1977-1981 term of the U.S. Carter Administration. The attrition continued, under a continuing influence of the Trilateral Commission during 1981-1987, but a steeply accelerated, further decline from the October 1987 echo of that 1929 stock-market-like crash which was followed by the still steeper decline of a collapsing U.S. economy, over the 1987-2007 interval.

This successively accelerated rate of decline, over the 1968-2008 interval, when seen in physical-economic terms, is fairly described as a turning back of the clock of human physical-economic and cultural development of the U.S. population (among others) in general. In effect, the clock of economic development, was running backwards. There has been an accelerating rate of decline of the U.S. economy and of the culture of the U.S. population, over that entire interval. *An extremely important kind of statistic!*

Unless we act to reverse that ratio of declining cultural human creativity interacting with decay in the basic economic infrastructure of society, mankind is going backwards.

This is not merely a correct statistical picture. The statistical picture, is a symptomatic correlative of the decay in the cultural morality of the society undergoing

ment of mathematics that we might finally understand the true principles of physics. The reason is that, among all creatures, only the human individual is capable of the creative reason on which all truthful discoveries of principle depend absolutely. That much said up to this point, we proceed now, as follows.

Keep that suggestion in mind. We shall consider it from a higher standpoint a bit later.

Take one of the simplest instances of the essential distinctions which draw a line between sane and moral persons on the one side, and the bestial sort of oaf on the other.

The Irony of Being Human

One of the ways in which to express the difference of man from the beasts, lies in the fact that the beasts, composing a dynamically defined bit of ecology, can temporarily overrun a normal, dynamic limit for a set of species cohabiting an environment; whereas, any healthy form of human society, tends toward a voluntarily permanent outrunning of any ecological limit which might be attributed to a mankind seen in terms of such a form of ongoing decadence. As I have described effects, the related question is, "Effects of what cause? Effects of what kind of action?"

The immediate answer by most thoughtful respondents to that challenge from me, is that it is this pattern of decline over the term of President Harry Truman, the continuation of the actual decline leading into the 1957-59 recession in the U.S.A. and in the United Kingdom during the 1950s, the decline in Europe in the late 1960s, the different modes of decline of the trans-Atlantic society during the 1970s and 1980s, and the accelerated, ultimately catastrophic decline of the 1989-2009 interval to present date.

The solution for that paradox, lies in a voluntary quality of the human personality which does not exist as a voluntary capability in any living creature but the human individual. This voluntary capability is what is properly identified as the creative powers of the human individual type, powers which do not exist in any other form of life. Here lies the distinction of what Academician Vernadsky identified as the true meaning to be assigned to the term "Noösphere," as distinct from the involuntary creativity which occurs as a dynamic potentiality (upwards genetic shift in evolution) within the lower forms of life.[7]

III. A War for Modern Scientific & Economic Creativity

Before getting to the core of what I have to say in the following, concluding chapter of this three-part presentation, I must prepare the way by reporting on something as a matter of relevant autobiographical background respecting the crucial point which I have to make before completing this chapter of the report.

My earliest commitment to Gottfried Leibniz, which occurred during my adolescence, and was expressed by a product of intensive study on every bit of Gottfried Leibniz to which I had access at that time. By early 1953, I was committed to the principles of Bernhard Riemann's 1854 habilitation dissertation, and some related writings. The entirety of my professional commitment to a science of physical economy, has embodied that commitment to the concept of history, from that

past time, in my adolescence, to the present moment.

Some decades later, about 1977, I came to adopt the work of Cardinal Nicholas of Cusa in his included role as the author of the founding of the modern science of such of his followers as Leonardo da Vinci and Johannes Kepler, and, thus, of the current of modern physical science which is typified by Pierre de Fermat, Christiaan Huyghens, Gottfried Leibniz, and such Leibniz followers as Jean Bernouilli, Lazare Carnot, and, especially Bernhard Riemann. The recognition of Cusa as the actual founder of the general principles of a competent modern physical science came about through my wife Helga's participation in a conference of the Cusanus Gesellschaft, and my ensuing proposal to her that she pursue her proposed doctoral preparation with emphasis on Cusa's work.

This attention to Cusa opened up my view of the whole sweep of modern European science, prompted by the work and role of Cusa and his immediate followers at the center of that process. It is when we trace the founding of competent modern physical science around the central figures of such followers of Cusa as Leonardo da Vinci, Johannes Kepler, and, also, Pierre de Fermat: that the entirety of the work of such as Christiaan Huyghens, Leibniz, and Jean Bernouilli, opens up for us in a much richer way than before, richer because we are thus better equipped to re-experience, rather than merely interpret, the relevant process of development from Filippo Brunelleschi, Cusa, and so on.

The particular relevance of that piece of background material in this present report, is that the comprehension of the relative superiority of the European Fifteenth and Sixteenth centuries' progress in scientific fundamentals, provides the occasion to understand more clearly, the elementary nature of the sheer fraud represented by that influence of Paolo Sarpi on which the subsequently dominant trends in leading forms of principled corruption of modern science were premised, as from the Seventeenth Century of Sarpi, Galileo, Descartes, and Abbé Conti onward. This conflict is essential to a clear understanding of the practical significance of the concept which is the focus of my attention here, the concept of *physical time,* as distinct from *clock time.*

For making this point and its relevance clear here, one should start with the uniquely original discovery of the Solar system's governing principle of universal gravitation as discovered by no other discoverer than

---

7. Contrary to the statisticians, biological evolution is not statistical in nature.

Johannes Kepler. In this matter, Kepler's adversaries Paolo Sarpi and his lackey Galileo, turned the clock of science backwards, in more ways than one. We must reset that clock, by proceeding as Albert Einstein understood, and emphasized the discovery of that principle of universal, physical space-time, which was to be promoted by Einstein himself. This was a discovery of principle, which had been on the knife's-edge verge of being identified by that work of Kepler completed just before his death from starvation. No other person than Kepler had actually discovered the principle of gravitation, then, or until the work of Bernhard Riemann produced the crucial changes which erupted at the outset of the Twentieth Century.[8]

The story which needs to be told, at least in brief, here, is the following.

Kepler's Discovery

The success of Kepler's discovery of the principle of universal gravitation, depended upon recognizing what lay in the functional intersection of two types of phenomena. One, was a mental image of the universe based on transforming the data into the terms of visualization of the image of their set of Solar orbits. The second, was conceptualizing the periodicities, which are distributed dynamically, among the sets of orbits in the fashion of musical harmonics, as the notion was seen by the specific succession of the Pythagoreans and Plato.

The challenge which came to be posed, thus, by the large accumulation of required studies of the orbits, posed, for Kepler, an image of that evidence which corresponded to an ironical juxtaposition of the image of vision and the images of musical harmonies. In short, vision and harmonics, as the instrument for study of the characteristics of the orbital system, became the principal illustrations of the experience to be resolved into a single conception; they identified the set of contrasting instruments whose paradoxical juncture served as the combinations needed to adumbrate the reality of gravi-

For Kepler, the challenge posed by the large accumulation of studies of the planetary orbits, required that he resolve, into a single conception, both the image of vision, and the image of musical harmonies.

tation itself. The use of instruments to investigate a set of phenomena which can not be regarded as being in itself a direct representation of the phenomenon being experienced, is not an unusual challenge in any work of discovery of principle in the domain of physical science. It was from this view of the evidence, evidence treated in this way, that Kepler discovered the principle of gravitation which was later fraudulently coopted as "Newton's discovery."

As I shall point out in this report, Kepler's insight into the existence of an unseen, unheard, but efficient, universal principle called universal gravitation, brought Kepler to the brink of a next step which would have established the concept of a physical universe, as ruled by a principle whose efficiency could not be premised on any specific human sense-organ, and which, therefore, could be known to the senses only through a certain quality of conflict between asymmetrically juxtaposed, relevant sense-experiences: which is to say, this array functioned as a physically efficient object of the human

---

8. The form of the principle of general gravitation, as discovered by Kepler, was not discovered by Isaac Newton. It was copied by the circles of the controllers of Newton from the previously published edition of some Kepler work. All that was added was a factor actually provided by the circles of Huyghens and Leibniz. As John Maynard Keynes proclaimed, on opening the mysterious secret chest of Newton papers, Newton discovered absolutely nothing of scientific interest, but chiefly just "black magic" of the witchcraft style.

All of the major wars in modern society have been based on the method of religious and related warfare, first introduced by the Spanish and Austrian Habsburgs during the religious warfare of 1492-1648. Peter Bruegel's "Triumph of Death" (1562, detail), captures the insanity and beastiality of the Religious Wars.

mind, not directly represented by any single sense-experience.

Such a discovery by Kepler, which we can recognize as having been implicit in his declared discovery of the principle of universal gravitation, was implicitly at the edge of the basis for discarding the notions of absolute space and absolute time, that in favor of *physical space-time.*

Those were conceptions which lurked, as shadows of a coming future discovery, in the discovery of refraction by Pierre de Fermat, and in Gottfried Leibniz's fulfillment of a challenge left to "future mathematicians" by Kepler. Such was, the calculus whose discovery, by Leibniz, was delivered in proof to a Paris printer some time between 1675-1676. Why, then, did the discovery of relativistic physical space-time wait until the announcement of Albert Einstein in the middle of the first decade of the Twentieth Century?

Ironically, Kepler had been in correspondence with the musician Vincenzio Galilei, the father of the notable Galileo Galilei, for assistance in collecting information on the musical scale and related matters. Kepler's purpose in that exchange was to compare the musical intervals corresponding to the characteristics of the Solar system's orbits. So far, all seems good, until the intervention of Galileo Galilei, who used information which

he drew from Kepler's correspondence with Vincenzio. There was an ugly irony in this. Galileo Galilei was an agent of the notorious Paolo Sarpi, who was the founder of all modern Liberalism, and an adopted follower of the medieval irrationalist, William of Occam.

The drama in fact which was represented on the stage of the history of empiricist science, by the players Kepler, Paolo Sarpi, Vincenzio Galilei and his son Galileo, is the key to understanding the source of the apparent difficulty which Einstein appears to have encountered in addressing the concept of physical time.

This Eighteenth Century's controversy over the issues, had been a problem which has continued to plague all of modern science since the Seventeenth-century influence of, most notably, the Liberals Sarpi, Galileo Galilei, Rene Descartes, Abbé Antonio S. Conti, and, later, Voltaire. All of these persons overlap, as Galileo is a creature of Sarpi, Descartes is a product of the doctrinal influence of Galileo, Conti is a devotee of Descartes and a key creator of the largely synthetic personality of Isaac Newton. Conti, and Voltaire, et al., are all collaborators in running a European network of Leibniz-hating salons featuring Abraham de Moivre, D'Alembert, Leonhard Euler, Euler's protégé Lagrange, and their followers Laplace and Augustin Cauchy. The key to all of them is Paoli Sarpi, the father of all modern European and related (Ockhamite) Liberalism.

However, it would be foolish to believe that those connections are merely connections. They are all bound together by a dynamic quality of common tie which defines them, each and all, as, functionally, a single thing, a species as common to all, as that of a kennel of dogs of the same breed. What unites all of them from the time of Conti's arrival in Paris and proclaiming himself as a Cartesian, is their determination to destroy, first, the influence of Nicholas of Cusa, Johannes Kepler, Fermat, and, then, Gottfried Leibniz. During the course of the Eighteenth Century, especially after the death of Leibniz, they were gathered around, first, Conti, and by the time Conti died (in 1749), Conti's follower Voltaire.

The common feature of all of them, was manifest by their common motive, their commitment to the eradication of the influence of Cardinal Nicholas of Cusa and of Gottfried Leibniz. The issue was the Leibniz infinitesimal; the more deep-rooted targets were Cusa, and Cusa's avowed followers Leonardo da Vinci, and Kepler.

The Role of Religious Warfare

Since Babylon, all of the known empires based in the land areas encompassing the Mediterranean Sea, have been based on the same principle of method which Edward Gibbon recommended to his patron, Lord Shelburne, the method of the infamous Roman emperor known as Julian the Apostate. It is the method expressed by the Pantheon of Rome, and by no means a tactic restricted to the wretched Julian; what is called "The British Empire" has always used religious conflict or comparable cultural hostilities as the way to rule, by pitting one subject—one religious faction, one social stratum, one ethnic origin—against the others.

All of the major wars in modern society have been based on the expression of the method of religious and related warfare, as this was introduced by the Spanish and Austrian Habsburgs during the religious warfare of 1492-1648, used by the dupes of Paolo Sarpi to organize the wars which engaged France's foolish Louis XIV, the Seven Years War, and by Napoleon Bonaparte, later. Britain's organizing of what became known as World War I, was initially organized by Prince of Wales Edward Albert, organized by causing the ouster of Germany's Chancellor Bismarck, then arranging the assassination of France's President Sadi Carnot, and then enlisting the Mikado to launch the Japan warfare against China which continued, with some very temporary interruptions, until Summer 1945. The decisive action by London in this process, was the assassination of U.S. President William McKinley, an assassination whose featured effect was to cause the United States to change sides, from prevalent popular sympathy for Germany and Russia, to favoring Britain in World War I. Out of World War I, came the Sykes-Picot arrangement, under which the British Empire has kept the religions of Southwest Asia at one another's bloody throat to the present instant.

This use of orchestrated religious and related conflicts, was not new. It was what the Empires of the East had done. It was the method of the Roman Empire and the Byzantine Empire, and was the method of religious warfare through which the Venetian financier controllers of the Habsburgs ruled Europe from the relevant point in the Fourteenth Century, with only a relatively brief interruption, until 1648. Furthermore, it was the British who organized what became known as "World War I" as a replay of the British orchestration of the Seven Years War, and as a replay of the way in which London used the fool Napoleon Bonaparte to unleash the more than a decade and a half of continuing general warfare on the continent of Europe, a continuation of Napoleonic wars of sheer economic looting, by means of whose effects the British Empire's reign was secured until President Abraham Lincoln led the victory over the British organization of a Civil War inside the U.S.A. itself.

It was not warfare alone that enabled empires to run for as long as they did. The siege of Troy was such a case. The Peloponnesian War was another. So was the folly of the Achaemenid Empire, in a war which was won by Alexander the Great after he went to his mother's people, in Cyrenaica, to organize the revolt, against Persia, in Egypt, which enabled Alexander to conquer Tyre and thus take over the Persian Empire.

So, in recent decades, Britain sought to destroy the United States by inducing the U.S. to forge a fraudulent pretext for entering a long, ruinous war in Indo-China, and so the evil British Prime Minister Tony Blair induced the foolish U.S. George W. Bush administration to take a course which wrecked the U.S.A. military, and the U.S. economy, by an unnecessary, ruinous long war in Southwest Asia. It is no surprise that former Vice-President Cheney was not acting as a patriotic American in luring a nasty and befuddled President George W. Bush to ruin the U.S.A., by luring the silly Bush into embracing Blair's fraudulent actions luring the U.S.A. into the ruinous long war in Southwest Asia. Similarly, the singularly unpatriotic Cheney was still trying to get Israel to destroy itself in an attack on Iran, practically up to the very last weeks of the now concluded Bush administration.

Similarly, actual and would-be imperial systems have used their orchestration of religious conflicts, to maintain control over the interior of an empire, which is why the largely brutalized, British population itself is, largely, so terribly unskilled, badly educated, and economically incompetent today, and why the anglophiles inside the U.S.A. have done so much to attempt to stupefy the U.S. population, as much as possible, by de-

The technological improvements prompted by Nicholas of Cusa's leadership in science and statecraft, could be seen among the populations of the cities whose culture had been influenced by the Renaissance. Here, the Dutch painter Jan Vermeer's "View of Delft" (1559-60).

industrializing the U.S.A. through exporting our production to cheap labor markets, spreading drug cults inside the U.S.A. and abroad, and making our nation's education and popular culture itself a farce.

Such were the considerations which guided Paolo Sarpi and his accomplices in launching their program of stupefying the people of Europe (in particular) into a state like the condition of the people of England which came to be described so aptly by Jonathan Swift's ***Gulliver's Travels***.

The 1618-1648 Warfare

That much said on those historical matters, now consider the strategic crisis which confronted the Habsburg rulers in the rise of the effects of that great Ecumenical Council of Florence led by such figures as the founder of modern physical science, the same Cardinal Nicholas of Cusa whose commitment to transoceanic outreach inspired the initial trans-Atlantic voyages of Christopher Columbus.

It was on this account that the Spanish Inquisition was launched as an international effort, that virtually in the same year as Columbus' first voyage in exactly the opposite geographic direction.

The relevant irony was that the intellectual revolution unleashed by the Fifteenth-Century Florence Council, had already begun to produce a great cultural uplifting of the people in Europe, as in Spain, Germany, France, and the Netherlands, which prevented the medieval-minded forces, under the Habsburgs, from securing durable victories over effectively determined resistance by the targeted populations. By the time of the close of the strategically disastrous Council of Trent, the Habsburg cause was effectively pre-doomed.

At that point, Paolo Sarpi had seized the opportunity created by the follies of Trent, to mobilize a rapidly growing political force in support of his new alternative program. He, in effect, at least, elected to virtually write off the cultures of the Mediterranean coast, and move his financier faction and its resources largely away from the Mediterranean littoral, to maritime bastions along the northern coasts, where the Protestant factions would be relatively dominant.

By the time of the end of the Council of Trent, it was already clear, as Niccolo Machiavelli, who had become the great strategist of his time, recognized the factors which showed that the Habsburg forces must tend to be defeated in the long run. The relevant factors included the effect of the Council of Florence in promoting the development of the culture away from the follies of the Thirteenth and Fourteenth centuries. This development included the technological improvements which were promoted by Nicholas of Cusa's leadership in science and related elements of statecraft. The new conditions were to be seen among the populations of the cities whose culture had been influenced by the Renaissance, which had made those populations a new kind of strategically effective factor, as Friedrich Schiller's analysis of the war in the Netherlands and the Thirty Years War had shown. Schiller's strategic insight was crucial then, as it was in guiding Scharnhorst's and related circles in designing the strategy which would, and did defeat Napoleon Bonaparte's war against Russia.

Sarpi, for his part, not only recognized, but was determined to exploit the fact, that the danger to the cause of the Venetian usurers' faction in Europe, lay in the progress of the population of Europe under the influence of the Renaissance and the consequent victories of Louis XI in France and his admirer, Henry VII in England. Sarpi's threatened dilemma was, that the northerly part of the Venetian interest would lose control of Europe if it accepted the Habsburg policy of suppressing the waves of scientific and technological progress which the Renaissance had unleashed; but, that it was to lose the fight in another way, if it permitted technical progress to be led by scientific progress of the type which the work of Johannes Kepler (in fact) typified. Sarpi's choice of middle ground, was to permit a certain degree of technological progress, of the types already under way in England and the Netherlands, but that Sarpi must lose if he did not prevent some degree of technological innovation from being a subsumed feature of the fundamental scientific progress which Cusa, Leonardo da Vinci, and Kepler typified.

So, Sarpi had dumped the Council of Trent's Aristotle, the prince of ancient and medieval darkness on that occasion, to allow some technological progress, but not to tolerate lightly a program of actually scientific progress in respect to principle.

The issue became acute for Sarpi's faction, when Cardinal Mazarin succeeded Richelieu in France. Mazarin initiated the feasibility of the 1648 Peace of Westphalia, while Mazarin's protégé, Jean-Baptiste Colbert organized support for a massive program of building an infrastructural and science-driver program for France. But, the foolish King Louis XIV fell into the trap of prolonged wars, and the British won the war through wars of the type culminating in the Seven Years War. So came that establishment of the British Empire, as a private empire of the British East India Company under Lord Shelburne's leadership.

After the 1648 Peace of Westphalia, there were now three principal, mutually opposing strategic forces in Europe: the old regime, associated with the greatly weakened Habsburg interest; Sarpi's faction; and, centered in the France of Jean-Baptiste Colbert, the economic and social policies which were the outgrowth of the renaissance associated historically with the circles of Cardinal Nicholas of Cusa and of such followers of the Cusa initiatives as France's Louis XI and England's Henry VII.

The fight was now centered, essentially, between the movement centered in the France of the policies of Mazarin and Colbert, against what was to emerge as the new composition of the enemy faction, the faction now organized around the Anglo-Dutch Liberal followers of Sarpi and Rene Descartes.

The Real World War Today

In the meantime, Sarpi and his followers proceeded with an increasingly vigorous war of empiricism against real science. The fake Anglo-Dutch science of brutish William of Orange, was summoned to that cause; with the death of Queen Anne, brutishness was the reality of the British Flag. The addled Isaac Newton was summoned to carry the guidon, which perhaps was all he was good for, and thus to lead the dupes to battle for the cause of empiricist imbecilities. With the 1689-1763 defeats of France and of the American forces centered around the remnants of the Winthrops and Mathers of Massachusetts, there gathered, more and more, around the energetic genius of Benjamin Franklin, the leaders of the effective resistance to the imperial tyranny now assembled around a Britain under the thumb of what the 1763 Peace of Paris defined as a private empire under the thumb of the British East India Company. The fight was essentially between the tradition of Leibniz and the Sarpian ideological tradition of Rene Descartes.

The American Revolution, fought, implicitly, as a

recurring, world-wide war, from 1776 through to the time of President Abraham Lincoln's victory over the imperial enemies of the U.S.A., in 1865, defined the essential, global strategic conflict as between the patriotic forces in and of the United States, as against our republic's typical chronic, traditional enemy of the U.S.A. which is known, traditionally, as "the British Empire," but, which is the neo-Venetian financier-oligarchical empire of the international, imperial faction constituted as the followers of the ideological financier-oligarchical power associated with the tradition of Paolo Sarpi.

It has become, since the British crushing of the earlier independence of the New England settlements, about 1689, a war against creativity, led by the followers of Paolo Sarpi, against the legacy of scientific creativity of, essentially, Plato, Cusa, Kepler, and Leibniz, against the imperial, monetarist policies centered in the reductionist ideology of Paolo Sarpi and his intrinsically usurious, Cartesian tradition expressed as the dupes of the Isaac Newton cult.

The American Revolution was fought, implicitly, as a recurring, worldwide war, from 1776 to the time of Lincoln's victory, in 1865, against the British Empire, which, in reality, is the neo-Venetian financier-oligarchical empire of the followers of Paolo Sarpi. Shown, "The Surrender of Cornwallis at Yorktown," 1781, by John Trumbull (1786-87).

IV. The Theses

Popular opinion about time is associated with the notion, that, despite our knowledge of changes in the universe we inhabit, even catastrophic ones, that universe remains a territory within which the kinds of changes which we can expect to experience, even the most calamitous we might have yet to imagine, are limited to the bounds of a relatively fixed repertoire, whether we presently know the full spread of that repertoire of possibilities, or not. That belief is, of course, false.

In that sense, we believe in the imagined immortality of real estate, as we believe a-priori, axiomatically, in the immortality of clock time. That belief is also false.

*The customary assumptions about space and time are often related to a seemingly instinctive, silly belief in the immortality of the idea of real estate. Most people in our culture have a lurking suspicion that real estate is in some way immortal, as property in itself, whoever, or whatever might be the nominal proprietor. For similar reasons, most people, especially most who believe in Heaven, also consider Heaven, or whatever, as a special kind of supernal real estate, as Owen Gingerich, author of the foreword to a recent English edition of Johannes Kepler's **New Astronomy**, has, falsely, suggested a notion of that sort.*

Those sorts of pathetic beliefs coincide, more or less exactly, with a permanently Cartesian view of a universe of mere clock-time.

*Nonetheless, contrary to conventionally silly beliefs, those among us who are sane and have left our minds open to the known essentials of scientific principles, believe implicitly in the immortality of the human soul, as Moses Mendelssohn echoed Plato's **Phaedo** on this account. The efficiency of the human soul is not confined, even in the mortal expression of our existence, to the bounds of this body. Rather, the ideas which are shared in shaping the unfolding development of society, such as great Classical musical compositions of their* *composers, and, more emphatically, the effect of that work of composition, of poetry, music, and physical scientific progress, and the experienced lessons of its performance, bear the mark of what had been the presence of the relevant persons. Thus, human beings who are truly alive while they are living in the flesh, are never merely packages of data, but are the expression of a personal power which transcends the bounds of their animal flesh.*

Plato and Mendelssohn are not speculating in this matter; their insights may not be perfect; but, they are true.

At bottom, it is the development of the human species in the way which corresponds to true Classical-artistic and scientific progress, which defines the meaning of our experience, and of our once having lived. Actually, the very possibility of the existence of mankind as a species, depends upon that kind of process of development, experienced in that way. These types of considerations, are the substance of our souls, that of our nation, for example, humanity generally, nations properly conceived, and of each of us personally. Think of the passage of time as, in a certain respect, like space, a distance travelled. Think of time as physical time, instead of as clock-time. We live temporarily but the better among us live on as immortals in a vast simultaneity of eternity.

That process of change to which we might contribute on behalf of that universe we inhabit so, when considered in such terms, reveals the real, essential content of the passage of physical time. This is not only an idea about us and our nations. It is the standard of reference for measuring the degree and rate of progress in the existence of the human species in this qualitatively changing universe which we, at this given moment, inhabit. It is time so measured, in the principle of anti-entropic action, not "clock time," which is real.

It is time to free ourselves from silly ideas, including the prevalent silly conception of "clock time" among the victims of this.

The evolution of species, whether species of the abiotic phase-space, or of the Biosphere, is an expression of an innately *anti-entropic* impulse, an impulse which resides within us, as an inherent potential of the dynamics of those two general categories of existence on our planet, and beyond. The crucial difference between the endemic creativity of the human species and those of the Biosphere, or the abiotic phase-space generally, is

that the development of mankind to higher levels of expressed anti-entropic development, such as evolutionary development of that quality, is consciously willful, or, at least, approximately so. Therefore, so far, knowledge of actual human creativity, has been limited to the cases of exceptional human individuals, but this need not remain so. We must come now to understand the significance of *physical time*.

Thus, although creativity is pervasive in the universe, as this is to be noted in the case of the evolutionary development of our planetary system from a relatively solitary Sun to a Solar system, we know only that creativity becomes efficiently conscious on Earth today only among human individuals, so far, only rarely. Nonetheless, it has been our great misfortune as a society, so far, that conscious recognition of that potentiality has been widely suppressed, *successfully*, among most in the known cultures of the planet thus far.

The unfortunately widespread suppression of knowledge of this potentiality, on our planet, so far, as such a kind of suppression is the subject of Aeschylus' **Prometheus Bound**, continues to be a great obstacle to the existence of popular understanding of the existence and function of *physical time*, as opposed to the illusory notion of *clock-time*.

Moreover, the suppression of knowledge of physical time, as distinct from mere clock time, has put humanity as a whole repeatedly at risk, by the suppression of the percentile of efficiently, consciously creative human individuals, to a small fraction of the human populations as a whole, so far.

For example, consider the currently widespread belief in the actually absurd concoction of the Nineteenth-Century hoaxsters, the formal mathematicians Rudolf Clausius and Hermann Grassmann who put forward, through Clausius, in 1850, the fantasy which became known later, through his associate Lord Kelvin, as the infamous "Second Law" of thermodynamics, and also became known as the "law of entropy." One should note that both Clausius and Grassmann were mathematicians, not physicists, and made a number of blunders which have tended to be typical of mathematicians; blunders of a type, verging on the effects of formalist *a-priorism*, which remind us of the necessity for the precious, concluding sentence, on the subject of mere mathematics, of Bernhard Riemann's 1854 habilitation dissertation.

Much of the worst effects of the types of systemic

errors which mathematicians have tended to perpetrate in modern society, when they have invaded the domain of physics, can be traced, in modern European practice, to the impact of Paolo Sarpi's influence in promotion of a revival of medieval William of Ockham's "razor." This depravity of theirs is characteristic of the ideology of Anglo-Dutch Liberalism and its like.

The problem of note is, that Sarpi had adopted Ockham's silliness as a way of, on the one hand, permitting practical inventions, but, at the same time, refusing, like the Olympian Zeus of Aeschylus' **Prometheus Bound**, to tolerate the discovery and propagation of actual physical principles. This is of particular note for reason of the fanaticism of the Venetian followers of Sarpi in their attacks on the work of such pioneers as Nicholas of Cusa and Cusa's follower Johannes Kepler. It is to be noted, for example, in the brutish intellectual character of the fraudulent claims against Gottfried Leibniz by fakers such as the Eighteenth-century hoaxsters Abbé Antonio Conti, Abraham de Moivre, D'Alembert, Leonhard Euler, and Euler's protégé Joseph Lagrange.

For example: A glance at the follies of de Moivre, D'Alembert, Euler, Lagrange, Laplace, and Augustin Cauchy on the subject of the uniquely original Leibniz discovery of the calculus, points toward what might be named the "purloined letter" of the case of their deliberate fraud against science. The attempt of these empiricist clowns of modern philosophical Liberalism, to deny the ontological actuality of the "infinitesimal" of the Leibniz calculus, is "keystone" evidence of the origins of the popularization of the fraudulent "second law of thermodynamics."[9] This is an important key for the understanding of the meaning of the term "physical time," as distinct from "clock time."

The empiricists' and Aristoteleans' denial of the existence of an *efficient infinitesimal* in the Leibniz calculus, is a key to understanding the nature, and importance of the distinction of *the anti-entropy of physical space-time* from the notion of entropy inherent within the arbitrarily presumed reductionist outlook of the followers of either Aristotle, or of Sarpi's attempted resur-

rection of the deceased Ockham.

The issues which I have just described in that way, can be properly referenced for further discussion by glancing at Einstein's emphasis on a finite but unbounded universe, a concept which he linked to the uniquely original discovery of universal gravitation by Kepler. Whereas the Liberal or Aristotelean mathematician sees only a formulation of a suggested physical principle, as locating the universe within the bounds of the fancied trajectory of some allegedly relevant mathematical formulation, on the contrary, Kepler's principle, as seen by Einstein as referencing a finite but unbounded universe, bounds the referenced mathematical function, as Kepler did, rather than being bounded by it.

This distinction has similar significance to the impossibility of bounding a circle or sphere by quadrature, as Euler did in his support of the Sarpian dogma against Leibniz. As Einstein emphasized, Kepler's discoveries of trajectories in astrophysics (and otherwise) bound the process described, in the same sense that universal gravitation, as originally, and uniquely discovered by him bounds a current value in astrophysics. Since that universe is developing, the universe is immediately finite, and, also, essentially anti-entropic.

The Folly of Clock-Time

The occurrence of phenomena such as novae within the astronomer's universe, such as that Crab Nebula which does much, periodically, to combat the radiation of the Sun in shaping some of the leading effects experienced in our own Earth, presents us with evidence of the "mortality" of both Solar systems and the galaxies which they inhabit. If entire galaxies must expect to experience such events, where can we expect to find hope for permanence of any particular existential condition in this universe? Yet, scientific experience has informed us of human scientific progress toward, ultimately, managing what may be seen today as presently awfully awesome powers beyond our presently developed capabilities as mankind.

When we reflect on such deeply underlying, presently awesome realities of human existence in this universe, we are guided by conscience to think differently than most governments, nations, and their individual people have come to think, habitually, today.

We who live today shall not "get there" in today's conventional reading of such language. What, then, shall we, who live now, and will die soon, achieve?

---

9. It should not be found astonishing that users of the term "thermodynamics" among the devotees of Clausius, Grassmann, and Kelvin, and Ernst Mach follower Ludwig Boltzmann, have no actual comprehension of the proper use of the term "dynamis" or "dynamics." Their use of the term is a form of ignorant blunder which constitutes evidence going to the heart of the issue of incompetence which I charge against those authors in respect to the notion of anti-entropy.

"The most relevant fact in the history of science, is the degree to which—when science prevails over un-science—mankind's power in and over the universe is increasing, as a trend." Here, a photo, from the Hubble Telescope, of overlapping galaxies.

Briefly, the answer is, our importance lies in the changes toward the greater powers of humanity which will be required to ensure that what we might contribute, with our mortal lives today, will have an assured, respectable outcome in contributing to the distant state of the universe which mankind must do much, in terms of our species' relative powers now, to pre-shape today. There, immortality appears as it truly is for us now, concretely: a *simultaneity of eternity.*

This brings us to the heart of the subject of physical, rather than clock time.

Economy & Physical Time

As I have remarked earlier here, the discovery of universal gravitation by Johannes Kepler established implied evidence which brought the achievements of Johannes Kepler to the verge of the related discovery of the principles of physical space and physical time. The obstacle to that further discovery was, chiefly, the grabbing of political power over science by the circles associated with the leadership provided by Paolo Sarpi, most notably Sarpi's relevant leading lackey, Galileo Galilei.

The most crucial aspect of that wrecking of modern science, was the introduction of the mechanistic method in mathematics for which Galileo was merely typical, together with the spread of the influence of the hoaxsters Rene Descartes and the avowed Cartesian of Paris-based, Venetian pedigree, Abbé Antonio Conti. The most crucial of the sly tricks involved in these hoaxes was the hysterical insistence, by the opponents of Kepler, Fermat, and Leibniz, on the empiricist's presumption that the "infinitesimal," as defined by the Leibniz discovery of the calculus, did not exist.

Although the entirety of the cult of the black-magic specialist Isaac Newton documented no physical research at all, the overt admission of that fact was the issue of the followers of Sarpi against competent science, which was uttered by a series of Eighteenth-century hoaxsters associated with the notorious Leibniz-hater Voltaire, such as France's Abraham de Moivre, D'Alembert, Leonhard Euler, and Euler's protégé Joseph Lagrange. As de Moivre himself formulated the hoax's pivotal assertion, the argument was that the efficient physical infinitesimal of Leibniz's discovery of the catenary-cued, *universal physical principle of physical least action*, depended upon the evidence of an allegedly "imaginary" magnitude. Euler's argument to this effect, in supporting the hoax by de Moivre and D'Alembert, was the most obvious case of crude, barefaced lying of the most blatant sort. Euler's hoax led to that of the Duke of Wellington's sometime assets, Laplace with his silly "three-body" concoction and the hoaxster, and plagiarist (as, explicitly, of the original work by Niels Henrik Abel) Augustin Cauchy.[10]

---

10. The crucial, allegedly missing paper by Abel, which Cauchy plagiarized, turned up, neatly catalogued in Cauchy's filing, showing that Cauchy had seized the opportunity of Abel's death to plagiarize that original work of Abel. Laplace and Cauchy came to power in France through the role of the Duke of Wellington who was the official representative of the occupying power in France, following the final defeat of Napoleon Bonaparte. The result was not only appointment of the

However, to understand how that fraud of the Eighteenth-century empiricists came into being, one has to look back toward the actual roots of empiricism in the work of Sarpi, Sarpi's resurrection of the slop of that medieval irrationalist William of Ockham. This is a typical case of the type in which a criminal incriminates himself by leaving behind thorough evidence of not only his criminal act, but proof of the criminal intent which preceded the act.

In the history of known Egyptian and European science since the program of *Sphaerics* associated with the Pythagoreans, Socrates, and Plato, the concept of leading science, had been discovery of universal physical principles validated by methods of what Riemann was to identity as *unique experiments, experiments whose success* defines universal and closely related principles of scientific work. In contrast to that competence, the fraud Laplace sought to simply destroy existing scientific evidence by unproven methods, an incompetence he sought to evade by manufacturing the hoax called "the three-body problem"—perhaps a celebration of the Duke of Wellington, Laplace, and Cauchy, all in the same bed.

In the comparable clinical case, of Sarpi's embrace of the medieval Ockham, Sarpi excluded physical-experimental proof (as such proof was exemplified by the work of such Cusa followers as Leonardo da Vinci and Kepler), in favor of certain types of apparent coincidences. If the concocted scheme could be caused to appear to be plausible, and Sarpi and his accomplices chose to profess that they admired it, it could be adopted, by aid of richly lying assertions contrary to reality.

The idea of "proof" which Sarpi's Ockhamite followers, the empiricists, employed came to be mathematical formulas decreed to be self-evidently plausible in the opinion of an influential set of hoaxsters, without any reference to experimental or comparable proof of principle. The entirety of all of what was claimed as "original work" of the Newton school and its followers of the Eighteenth and Nineteenth Centuries, was of that cast. Thus, mathematical formulas were crafted and employed as substitutes for crucial kinds of experimental principles. On the basis of that method, actual principles, such as the principle of universal gravitation discovered by Kepler, were denied in a completely arbitrary way.

The most consequential aspect of such frauds by the empiricists, mechanists (such as Ernst Mach), and worse positivists (such as Bertrand Russell, Norbert Wiener, and John von Neumann), have that common feature.

It was the latter reductionist methods, which came to political power through the establishment of Sarpi's influence expressed in the contemporary ideology of the virtually world-wide British (drug-pushing, financier-oligarchical) empire, which used that power of imperial financier practices, such as the financial-derivatives frauds which have bankrupted the world's financial-monetary system today, to achieve a world empire of Venetian-style oligarchical-financier power.

From the standpoint of natural law, the crucial feature of the imperial system which has recently entered the final phase of its existence as a breakdown-crisis of the present world financial system, is its prohibition against any systemic consideration of the principles of physical economic practice on which the immediate continuation of civilized life upon this planet now immediately depends.

The Function of Physical Time

When the case against imperial financial systems is taken into account, and considered in the terms of reference which I have chosen, especially so, at the outset of this present chapter of the report, the fragility of the false presumption that the planetary and interplanetary systems of today are the permanent form of experience for the mind of the members of the human species, points our attention to the challenge of ensuring the continuity of what mankind so far has been building. Then, rather than imagining that the stage of the universe in which we stand now, will be a permanent setting for the human soul; we must think of how

---

British asset who became, thus, the new King of France, to replace the previous leading candidate, France's national hero Lazare Carnot, but the British use of their stooge, the new Bourbon monarch, to wreck the educational program which had created the Ecole Polytechnique associated with both Gaspard Monge and Carnot. The hoaxsters Laplace and Cauchy were assigned to replace the Monge and Carnot, who had created and headed the Ecole as the leading scientific institution of the world during that time. Alexander von Humboldt, who had been a close associate of Carnot in the Ecole Polytechnique, did much to rescue and advance the Ecole's work, despite Laplace and Cauchy. This collaboration with Alexander von Humboldt, led to the launching of *Crelle's Journal*, the first of a series of similarly intended ventures which played a decisive role in the advance of science during that century.

"When one's immortal package has been emptied of the animal we inhabited, and now must cast aside, it is what our mind has become as a power to defend, and to improve the universe, which becomes the replacement for some poor animal's notion of time." Here, memebers of the LaRouche Youth Movement in Germany explore the principles of the physical universe.

thing is anti-entropic development. This means emphasis on the relative rates of development of man's powers and condition, and that relative to the entropy which the so-called malthusians require, which would gobble us up, and make the future existence of man like that of the former Dodo. The rate of development, relative to attrition, and the outcome of progress so defined, now replaces mere abstract notions of a-priori space and a-priori time, with net rate of qualitative powers of fundamental scientific progress to higher states of being.

The development of human space-time, a development within which the death of the mortal package occurs within which we are delivered to us, is the measure of the meaning of the spiritual existence of each among us all. After all, when one's immortal package has been emptied of the animal we inhabited, and now must cast aside, it is what our mind has become as a power to defend, and to improve the universe, which becomes the replacement for some poor animal's notion of time.

we must build the development of that which is incarnated as spiritually, within us, such that the purpose of those souls which we are, shall become adapted to our future circumstances under which the distant future changes in the composition of our universe will continue to supply meaning to what we have been up to now.

In this view of immortality as a purpose for mankind's existence, time as we have been accustomed to discussing it formerly, now has a changed quality for truly sane mankind. Time and space become complementary, if essential parts of the total experience; but, as Einstein's circles emphasized, already, at the beginning of the Twentieth Century, time by itself, and space by itself, are delusions which no longer exist in that way.

What we must measure, therefore, is the rate of development of change of both the universe we inhabit now, and in the future when the circumstances may be qualitatively different. Thus, it is development of mankind, including man's changes in the organization and composition of our habitat, which is crucial. Clock time as such is of no intrinsic importance; the important

This conception which I have just summarized in that way, is possible for us, as not for the lower forms of life, because we have the power of true creativity, if we develop and use it. This power is represented, in its potential, as the uniqueness of the human's ability to make fundamental discoveries of principle, discoveries which change the universe we inhabit. It is the rate at which we progress in service of that intention, which is the measurement which supersedes that passage of clock-time which was never better than a relic of our species' sometimes bestial past.

It is that which we must measure, and forecast, if this planet is now to escape from the onrushing plunge, already under way in an advanced state of crisis. I suspect, on excellent premises, that Albert Einstein would agree.